Parenting a Defiant Child

PARENTING A DEFIANT CHILD

A Sanity-Saving Guide to Finally Stopping the Bad Behavior

Philip S. Hall, Ph.D.
Nancy D. Hall, Ed.D.

American Management Association

New York • Atlanta • Brussels • Chicago • Mexico City • San Francisco •
Shanghai • Tokyo • Toronto • Washington, D.C.

This publication is designed to provide accurate and authoritative information in regard to the subject matter covered. It is sold with the understanding that the publisher is not engaged in rendering legal, accounting, or other professional service. If legal advice or other expert assistance is required, the services of a competent professional person should be sought.

Library of Congress Cataloging-in-Publication Data

Hall, Philip S.
    Raising a defiant child : a sanity-saving guide to finally stopping the bad behavior / Philip S. Hall and Nancy D. Hall.
        p. cm.
    Includes index.
    ISBN 978-0-8144-0907-7
    1.   Child rearing. 2.   Parenting. 3.   Discipline of children. 4. Parent and child.   I. Hall, Nancy D., 1951–   II. Title.

    HQ769.H2517 2007
    649'.64—dc22

                                                    2007020974

Printing number

10 9 8 7 6 5 4 3 2 1

To Mary Delaney, an extraordinary parent.

CONTENTS

INTRODUCTION

All parents wonder from time to time whether they should be concerned about their child's noncompliance and defiance. It's a difficult call. Some level of noncompliance and even defiance is normal, particularly during the "terrible twos." Learning to oppose the will of others is, under certain circumstances, even healthy.[1] The problem is when the terrible twos continue on and on, and the amount of noncompliance and level of defiance increases. If this describes your child, there is reason for concern.

Your concern probably prompts you to ask, "Is it time to take action? Do I need to do something, maybe even something pretty drastic, to end my child's noncompliance and defiance?" Possibly. If your child is 3 years old or older, ask these questions:

1. Does my child frequently provoke other people?
2. Does my child intentionally defy me?
3. Does my child maliciously antagonize and fight with his or her siblings?
4. Does my child throw a temper tantrum when he doesn't get his way?
5. Do I let my child get away with things so I can have some peace and quiet?

If you answered yes to two or more of these questions, it is time for action. Children who are noncompliant and defiant at an early age seldom outgrow it.[2] Their outbursts, noncompliance, and defiance increase, to the point that the child is disrupting the entire household and stressing your marriage. Furthermore, such children have problems at school and elsewhere in the community. You must act.

But what to do? Some "experts" say that a child's defiant behavior is deliberate. Believing this, these experts tell parents that what the child needs is a healthy dose of firm discipline. One parent told me of a conversation with such a counselor. After the mother described her child's behavior, the counselor said, "The first thing you need to understand is that when the child wins, you lose. Your kid needs to learn who is in charge. He must come to realize that when you tell him what to do, you mean business!"

We do not agree with either that assessment of the problem or the solution. No child wakes up one day and decides to become noncompliant, defiant, and aggressive. Rather, children gradually become noncompliant and defiant for a variety of reasons. Some children display behavior problems in response to being raised in a stressful situation. Behaving badly is their attempt to cope. From the child's point of view, aggression is essential for self-preservation. Other defiant children are rewarded, albeit unintentionally, for their insistence on getting their way. For them, not complying and being defiant pays off. Then there are the defiant children who were born cranky. They arrived into the world with the kind of disposition that is a lifelong handicap for them and a problem for the people around them.

But the bottom line is that these children are not noncompliant, defiant, and aggressive because they enjoy tormenting their parents. They are defiant and aggressive because they cannot read social cues. These children are not belligerent because they like to offend people. They are belligerent because they lack impulse control. These children are not aggressive because they enjoy being mean. They are aggressive because they do not know any other way to get what they want.

The truth is that at a young age defiant children are already failing at life's most important task—learning how to have mutually rewarding relationships. These children do not need parents who try to punish them out of their noncompliance and defiance. Rather, these children need nurturing parents who have empathy for their children and the know-how to help their children develop and sustain meaningful relationships. To accomplish this, parents of children with challenging behaviors need new skills. But at this point, we must be perfectly candid. When raising a child with challenging behaviors, there are no easy answers or quick fixes. It is work. If possible, find other parents who are in a similar situation. Jointly read this book chapter by chapter, discussing the book as you go. Most importantly, assist and support each other as you learn new ideas and then implement them.

This book lays out the techniques and skills that, when implemented, will enable you to transform your relationship with your child from confrontational to harmonious. In this book, you will learn how to provide your child the structure and support he or she needs to behave appropriately. You will also learn how to use those instances of appropriate behavior to strengthen your relationship with your child, which is the antidote for ending your child's behavior problems.

ACKNOWLEDGMENTS

We are indebted to friends and colleagues who read early drafts of this book. They made valuable suggestions and contributions that enhanced the book's readability. In particular, we would like to thank Fay Jackman for editing the first draft of this book and helping to put the manuscript in a form that drew the attention of several publishing companies. We also thank Dr. Tom Stanage, an uncommonly gifted clinical psychologist, who made suggestions and offered advice that helped us better address the concerns and worries of parents. In addition, Dan Mayer, Shawn Huss, and Terry Tucker read particular chapters and gave us sound advice.

Parenting a Defiant Child

Part I

PREVENTION

Many books about parenting defiant children focus on how to discipline children when they are behaving inappropriately. Such books take a reactive approach to parenting. They tell you how to dole out punishment when your child behaves badly. But these books don't tell you the most important thing. They don't tell you what you can do so that your child will behave appropriately in the first place.

Years of working with defiant children and their parents have convinced us that the child's noncompliance, defiance, and aggression are but one side of the coin. The other side of that coin is the face of a dejected child who feels unvalued and frustrated. It is this discouraged child who needs your support and attention. For when this child comes to feel valued and unconditionally loved, he will not be defiant.

Ben Franklin was right when he said, "An ounce of prevention is worth a pound of cure." Accordingly, Part I of this book is about prevention—the things you can do to establish the special conditions that your defiant child needs so that she can be the child that you aspire for her to be.

1

Getting Started

A Distraught Mother

"My name is Maria Delgado," said a nervous voice at the other end of the phone. "I need help with my son Justin."

"How old is Justin?"

"Five."

"What kind of help do you and your son need?"

"Justin started kindergarten this fall. For a while things went well. But now the school is telephoning me every day. The principal tells me that Justin is having a bad day, and I have to come get him right away. But where do I take him?" Mrs. Delgado asked, her voice starting to break.

"Is your immediate problem where to take Justin when the school expels him for the day?"

"Yes, because I have to get back to work."

"Can you take him to a daycare program?"

"No. Justin has been kicked out of every daycare in town. Today, my boss told me that if I keep leaving work for family emergencies, he is going to have to let me go. I just don't know what to do. Can you help?" Mrs. Delgado asked, starting to cry.

Parenting a child like Justin is exasperating, humiliating, and discouraging. Children like Justin are noncompliant. When a parent makes a request, they don't comply. If the request is repeated, the child becomes defiant, often screaming "No" at the top of his lungs or casting a look that says, "Don't push it." If you do push it and say, "You will do it, or else . . ." the child becomes aggressive. He tips over a chair, throws a toy at you, and even hits, kicks, and bites if you attempt to enforce the "or else."

To make parenting even more difficult, many defiant children are also impulsive. Without thinking of the consequences, they do dumb things, like Jack who spread the baby's talcum powder on the wood floor so he could run and slide through it. Or when 5-year-old Sally said to the neighbor lady, who came over for pie and coffee, "No wonder you are so fat. You eat too much." Defiant children also sometimes do mean things. Like 10-year-old Rusty, who saw a boy riding his bike by the house and shot him with his paint-ball gun.

Defiant children refuse to do what their parents ask. When their parents tell them that it's bedtime, such children shout back, "No! I'm not going to bed. I'm watching TV." If the parents try to put the child in bed, she has a temper tantrum. So to buy a little peace and quiet, the parents let her play until she eventually and finally falls asleep on the floor.

Children with behavior problems also have a hard time playing with friends. Often as not, they play nicely for about fifteen minutes, and then some little thing erupts into a fight. If you have such a child, going to the grocery store or to the mall can be a nightmare. It's not uncommon for the child to demand a candy bar while you are paying the clerk for the groceries. When you don't immediately respond to the child's demand, he swipes his hand along the candy rack, spilling candy bars all over the floor and then screams at the top of his lungs, "I want candy. I want candy."

Defiant children also have problems at school. They get into scuffles with other children during recess, often losing their recess privileges. They don't follow the teacher's directions, and they don't get their desk work done. Worse, they disrupt the classroom, making it hard for other students to do their work.

Unfortunately, many parents of defiant children think they are the only ones in the entire community (if not the whole world) who have such a child. In their minds, everyone else's children are compliant, respectful, and obedient. Well, that just isn't true. Between 5 to 10 percent of children are markedly noncompliant, defiant, and aggressive. You are not alone. Don't let embarrassment keep you from helping your child.

BUT WHERE TO START?

The first question that parents of children with behavior problems ask is, "What can I do to stop my child from being behaving so badly?" It is a reasonable question, and one that needs to be answered—eventually. But don't start by asking, "What can I do TO my child to stop her bad behavior?" Rather, start by asking, "What can I do FOR my child so she will behave better? There are three critical first steps.

STEP ONE: STOP BLAMING YOURSELF

Parents of children who misbehave usually believe that they are the root cause of the child's behavior problems. So they blame themselves. But their guilt does not help their child behave better. In fact, some parents feel so guilty about their child's behavior problems that they are frozen into inaction. "I can't do anything to my poor child," they tell themselves, "because it's my fault!"

To complicate matters, even when parents don't blame themselves, others do.

"It's Your Fault!"

"Brandon had been in school only a week," Mrs. Larson informed the parent-training group, "when I got a phone call from the teacher. She asked me to meet with her after school. I asked her why, and she said it was because Brandon was behaving terribly in her class."

"When I got to the school, they were waiting for me—the teacher, the school psychologist, the special education director, and the principal. The teacher started first. She gave a minute-by-minute account of Brandon's behavior in the classroom and on the playground. She made Brandon seem like a monster. But that was not the worst of it. The worst of it was when the principal said, 'And we all know the cause of Brandon's behavior problems. If you would discipline Brandon at home, he wouldn't behave this way at school.'"

Many parents of children with behavior problems have been in Mrs. Larson's shoes, finding themselves being blamed for their child's conduct problems. The guilt that a parent feels is sometimes imposed by total strangers.

Give That Kid a Good Spanking

"Last week I took Rusty grocery shopping," Mrs. Paulson related. "He behaved pretty good [sic] as we went up and down the aisles. Rusty was still behaving himself when I pushed the cart into the checkout line. As I stood there waiting to have my groceries checked, Rusty saw the candy bars."

'I want a candy bar!' he demanded. As I was thinking about it, Rusty grabbed a handful of candy bars and threw them into the grocery cart.

'Stop that!' I said. Instantly, Rusty swiped his hand across the shelf, knocking dozens of candy bars onto the floor.

A stranger standing behind us grabbed the back of Rusty's jacket. Holding Rusty so that only his toes touched the floor, the stranger said, 'Here is your spoiled brat. Now give him the spanking that he needs.'"

Blaming parents does not help. It only drives them into isolation, putting up a barrier that makes it hard for parents to seek help. Furthermore, parenting techniques are only one factor impacting a child's behavior. Children's behavior is also determined by their temperament, and temperament is determined by heredity.[3] When they were only weeks old, many defiant children were whiny, fussy, easily upset, irritable, and hard to console. They were born with a difficult temperament that predisposed them from day one to respond to the world with noncompliance, defiance, and aggression. Raising a child with a difficult temperament is a challenge. Since it is impossible to change the child's temperament, the best parents can do is to help their child learn how to manage his or her fractious disposition.

Unfortunately, it seems that in our society when something is not perfect, something or someone has to be to blame. This necessity to find a scapegoat applies to children who have problems learning to read as well as to children who have behavior problems. This poem by an unknown author makes the point:

The Little Rascal

Said the college professor,
"Such rawness in a student is a shame.
Lack of preparation in high school
is to blame."

Said the high school teacher,
"Good heavens, that boy's a fool.
The fault, of course, is with the
Grammar school."

The grammar school teacher
Said, "From such stupidity
May I be spared. They sent
Him up to me so unprepared."

The primary teacher huffed,
"Kindergarten blockheads all.
They call that preparation?
Why it's worse than none at all."

The kindergarten teacher said,
"Such lack of training never
Did I see. What kind of
Woman must that mother be?"

The mother said, "Poor helpless
Child. He's not to blame.
His father's people
Were all the same."

Said the father
At the end of the line.
"I doubt the Rascal
Is even mine."

Step Two: Get The Diagnosis Right

Many children who display excessive noncompliance, defiance, and aggression have what mental health professions call Oppositional Defiant Disorder.[4] Indeed, noncompliance, defiance, and aggression are so strongly associated with Oppositional Defiant Disorder that many people think that all children who are noncompliant, defiant, and aggressive have Oppositional Defiant Disorder. That thinking often leads to misdiagnosis.

A Television Diagnosis

"Peter was my first child," Mrs. Jackman told the parent behavior-training group during its first meeting, "so I didn't have much to compare him to until, three years later, Jennifer was born. Then, I suddenly realized that Peter was not your typical child. I started wondering what was wrong.

"One morning I was watching the *Montel Williams Show* while I cleaned up after breakfast. He had a couple on the program that showed a homemade video of their child. The kid wouldn't do as he was told. When his dad tried to make him mind, the kid had a big tantrum. Peter acts just like this child, I thought.

"Then an expert came on. The expert, I think he was a psychiatrist, said that the child had Oppositional Defiant Disorder. Right then I knew that Peter had that same thing."

For other parents, it was the daycare provider or an educator who informed them that their child had Oppositional Defiant Disorder. Many times, such well-intended people are right and their advice is helpful. But just as often, they are wrong. Making the correct diagnosis of a child's behavior disorder is difficult. A child's noncompliance, defiance, and aggression might be due to Oppositional Defiant Disorder. But the non-compliance, defiance, and aggression can also be due to Asperger's Syndrome, Attention-Deficit/Hyperactivity Disorder, Bipolar Disorder, Depression, Fragile X, Generalized Anxiety Disorder, or Obsessive Compulsive Disorder, just to name a few.

It is not noncompliance, defiance, and aggression per se that determines what type of behavior disorder the child has. Instead, the diagnosis depends on such things as the conditions that elicit these conduct problems, their intensity, the purpose of the conduct problems, and the age of onset. To complicate the picture, the diagnosis of a childhood behavior disorder is also diagnosed, in part, by physical characteristics and in some cases, such as Fragile X, a chromosome analysis, which requires drawing a sample of the child's blood in order to look for irregularities among any of the 46 chromosomes found in each of our cells. The point is this: Making the correct diagnosis of the underlying cause of a child's excessive noncompliance, defiance, and aggression is not easy. It is the job of experts. The professionals best equipped for making the diagnosis are child psychiatrists, developmental pediatricians, and clinical psychologists who specialize in childhood behavior disorders.

> ## KEY CONCEPT
> Children with serious behavior problems should be seen by a professional in order to get the correct diagnosis.

If your child is markedly defiant, identifying the underlying cause of this behavior is critical. It is critical because diagnosing the underlying cause determines the best intervention. To use a medical example, if the physician finds that the child has a fever, is listless, and has a sore throat, she suspects that the child has a strep infection. But a number of things can cause fever, listlessness, and a sore red throat. So the prudent physician takes a throat culture and checks it for the presence of streptococci. If the culture contains streptococci, the physician prescribes an antibiotic. The antibiotic kills the bacteria, the symptoms disappear, and the child is cured. The correct diagnosis led to the right treatment.

Similarly, it is important to make the correct diagnosis of your child's behavior disorder. That way, you and the child will get the benefit of the correct medications and targeted behavioral interventions. For example, if the reason for your child's noncompliance, defiance, and aggression turns out to be Depression, a prescription for an antidepressant is one aspect of a good intervention. But while an antidepressant is the right intervention for defiance and aggression due to Depression, an antidepressant is not the right intervention for noncompliance and aggression stemming from Asperger's.

A thirty- to sixty-minute office visit is usually sufficient for the specialist to diagnose a child's behavior disorder. If the referral is recommended by your family physician, health insurance will generally pay the cost. But regardless of who pays, it is money well spent.

> **KEY CONCEPT**
>
> The correct diagnosis, which can usually be made in one office visit, leads to the most appropriate and useful interventions.

As a guideline, an evaluation is warranted if your child is noncompliant, defiant, and aggressive and if two or more of these descriptors fit:

- The child is 3 years old or older, and the behaviors have persisted for longer than six months.
- The child's outbursts are unpredictable.
- The smallest, least little thing can set off a huge outburst.
- The child attempts to harm or talks about harming self, others, or pets.
- The child has done extensive property damage to the house or items in the house.
- The child is unusually active, has trouble sustaining attention, and is impulsive.
- The daycare and preschool providers or school teachers have repeatedly voiced concerns about the child's behavior.
- You feel at your wit's end, having tried many approaches without success.

An evaluation sometimes determines that the child's noncompliance and defiance is not the entire picture. Many children who have Oppositional Defiant Disorder also have another disorder such as Asperger's Syndrome, Obsessive-Compulsive Disorder, and particularly Attention-Deficit/Hyperactivity Disorder. In fact, 30 percent of the children with Oppositional Defiant Disorder also have Attention-Deficit/Hyperactivity Disorder (ADHD).[5] Fortunately, ADHD responds favorably to medication.[6] Diagnosing and successfully treating ADHD significantly lessens the child's impulsive behaviors, and enhances his ability to meet his parents' expectations. This accomplished, both the parent and the child realize that with continued effort things can and probably will get better. On the other hand, if the ADHD is not diagnosed and thus left untreated, children with behavioral problems will not respond to even the best parenting techniques. Disappointed and discouraged, the parents and their child stop trying, and they also give up on each other.

There is yet a third reason that a child with behavior problems should be examined by a specialist. The evaluation probably will include an assessment of the stress that the child is putting on you, on your family, and on the school. If that stress is excessive, the specialist can offer a range of supportive services.

STEP THREE: LOOKING AFTER NUMBER ONE

As a commercial jet taxies toward the runway, the flight attendant gives the passengers a safety briefing. Part of the briefing goes like this: "In the event of a sudden loss of cabin pressure, a plastic bag will automatically descend from the overhead luggage container. Grab the mask, pull it down, and place the mask firmly over your face. Oxygen will begin flowing. Put on your own mask before you assist others." The last directive is particularly important. The flight attendant is telling the adults to attend to their need for oxygen before helping their children. The implication is clear. If parents do not first meet their need for oxygen, both they and their child are apt to die.

The same advice applies to parents raising a behaviorally challenged child. Before setting out to deal with your child's behavior problems, you must deal with the issues threatening your well-being and impairing your ability to be an effective parent. Specifically, this means that you must deal with one of the known risk factors for children to become noncompliant and defiant—parental stress.[7]

PARENTAL STRESS

Early on in each parent-training group, we ask the parents to complete the Parent Stress Index, a commercially marketed rating form.[8] Invariably, the parents in our parent-training groups are highly stressed.

Stress, particularly at high levels, brings out the worst in us. Stress decreases our ability to do tasks that require clear thinking, and stress also reduces our capacity for emotional control—such as is required when dealing with a child's temper tantrums. Therefore, it is important that you examine your stress level. Your ability to be the parent that you want to be depends on you keeping the stresses impacting your life at a manageable, nonoverwhelming level.

> **KEY CONCEPT**
>
> Parents must deal with their stressors before setting out to help their children.

Stressors can be put into one of two categories. Category I is for stressors that can be significantly reduced if appropriate actions are taken. For example, a parent who is clinically depressed can get treatment that will significantly reduce that stressor.

Category II is for stressors that are nearly impossible to eliminate. For example, being a single parent is an acute stressor, but there is no easy immediate remedy. Therefore, single parents must examine how that particular stressor is affecting their ability to parent, and they must then find ways to shield the child from its impact.

The research has shown that the following stressors put children at risk for developing behavior problems. Consider each of the known stressors and determine whether it is impacting your ability to parent. Self-evaluation is never easy, but if you are going to put yourself in a position that you can help your child, it is essential that you identify the stressors making it hard for you to be the best parent that you can be, and then make a plan for dealing with those stressors.

CATEGORY I STRESSORS: REDUCE THEM

MARITAL PROBLEMS

A stressed marriage puts children at risk for becoming noncompliant and defiant.[9] So if there are gnawing problems in your marriage, counseling has the potential to make a positive impact on your child's behavior. If your spouse is reluctant to go, try reframing the problem. Instead of saying that the marriage is the problem, start with the more immediate issue—the child. You might say, "Honey, Danielle's behavior concerns me. I think it would benefit her if we got some guidance in this area." This is true, and it's a good reason in itself to go to counseling. If there are additional problems in the marriage, they will emerge in the course of the counseling. If your spouse still refuses counseling, go alone.

Marital problems per se do not negatively affect children. What adversely affects children is watching and listening to their parents bicker, argue, and fight.[10] So if you and your spouse decide that marriage counseling would be useful, while you are in counseling, shield your children from your arguments and disagreements.

Depression

Mothers of defiant children are at particular risk for Depression.[11] The symptoms of Depression in adults are:[12]

- Listlessness
- Feelings of despair
- Constriction of interests
- Lack of energy
- Waking up early in the morning and being unable to fall back to sleep
- Feelings of worthlessness
- Weight loss

If you have two or more of these symptoms for longer than two months and cannot identify a physical reason for them, bring the symptoms to a physician's attention. If the cause is Depression, there are medications that offer considerable reduction in the symptoms, and medication in combination with talk therapy usually provides long-term relief.[13]

Alcohol and Drug Abuse

Parents who abuse alcohol and/or drugs put their children at risk to develop conduct problems.[14,15] Unfortunately, in our culture there is a fuzzy line between moderate use and abuse. Here are some guidelines:

- If using a mood-altering substance is part of your daily routine, it is possible that you have a substance-abuse problem.

- If you attempt to hide the use of the substance from others, it is likely that you have a substance-abuse problem.

- If you become agitated when anything or anyone interferes with your getting that drink or ingesting that substance, it is almost certain that you have a substance-abuse problem.

ISOLATION

Parents of defiant children often become isolated from their community and even from their natural support group.[16]

Mrs. Larson's Isolation

"My parents live only 40 miles away," Mrs. Larson told the parent-training group. "For the first five years of my marriage, we saw my parents several times a month. We played lots of cards, laughed, and became good friends. Then Brandon was born. At first, my mother was here all of the time, helping me with Brandon. Mom continued to help me while Brandon went through the terrible twos. But when Brandon never outgrew the terrible twos, Mom stopped helping. Now, Brandon is 8 and we hardly ever see my parents. When I invite them to our house, they always have an excuse."

"My in-laws live out of state. They visited us last summer. They were going to stay four days. We were planning on taking them fishing and boating. But after two days, they suddenly left. The last thing my mother-in-law said was, "You must be an awful mother, or why else would my grandson be so terribly spoiled!"

"A few years ago, we often got a sitter and went out to dinner and a movie. But no more. We can't get a sitter. None of them want to be responsible for Brandon. Even Jim, my husband, is home less and less. More and more, he spends his free time fishing, hunting, or having a beer with the guys from work. So I am home alone—I and Brandon, and we are to the point that we can't stand each other."

Mrs. Larson was isolated from her friends and even her family. She no longer had a support network, and her marriage was strained. She even started to resent Bandon. While she never said it, Mrs. Larson was questioning her ability to be an effective parent.

Don't slide your feet into Mrs. Larson's shoes. You cannot allow your child's behavior problems to isolate you from your family, your friends, and your community. If you have become isolated, you must immediately start getting reconnected. The first step is to get respite, meaning time away from your child. Perhaps another family member will take your child at specific times each week. For example, the child's uncle may take his son and your son on a Saturday outing. But do whatever it takes! You cannot be the parent you want to be if you don't keep connected with your friends and in touch with the community.

CATEGORY II STRESSORS: LESSEN THEIR IMPACT

SINGLE PARENTING

If you are a single parent, your child is at increased risk of becoming non-compliant and defiant.[17] As a single parent, your main stressor is that you are constantly on the job. You are the breadwinner, the homemaker, the repairman, the housekeeper, and the disciplinarian. It's exhausting.

An Overburdened Father

Tom was a goal-oriented, hard-driving single parent with a 7-year-old daughter, Sally. In addition to being a full-time college student, Tom worked two part-time jobs, getting no benefits from either.

To manage, Tom regimented every minute of his day with military precision. In the morning, Tom woke Sally at 6:15 sharp. By 6:25, Sally was to be dressed and to be downstairs for breakfast. After breakfast, Sally had five minutes to brush her teeth and put on her coat. By 6:45, Tom and Sally were on their way to the sitter's, allowing Tom to get to his job by 7:15. From the sitter's house, Sally walked to school. After school, Sally walked back to the sitter's. Dad picked her up at 9:10. At home, Sally immediately took a bath. She was in bed by 9:30.

Often, single parents are so busy coping that they cannot find the time to do fun, relationship-building things with their children. But to children, any attention is better than no attention. To get attention, the children of overly busy parents often act out, even if their inappropriate behavior results in them being yelled at or harshly disciplined. For example, a single parent is busy getting dinner ready but her 5-year-old is shouting for her to come play ball. The parent ignores him. Soon, he starts throwing the ball against the wall, and it bounces into a table lamp, knocking it over. The parent runs into the room. Grabbing her son by the arm, the parent says, "Stop that! Stop throwing that ball this instant!" The child may stop throwing the ball, but he got what he wanted—his mother's attention. Unfortunately, he got attention in a way that further strained the parent–child relationship.

Because single parents are overburdened and often exhausted, they can find it physically hard to be consistent in their disciplining practices. When you are worn out emotionally and physically, it is not surprising that sometimes you ignore what your child is doing, even if the behavior is unacceptable. But at other times, your child does the very same thing and you punish her. This inconsistency in your disciplining practices wreaks havoc on your self-concept. A few moments after ignoring the child's unacceptable behaviors, you see yourself as allowing your child to get away with anything and everything. You're a wuss who can't control your offspring. But when you dole out harsh, anger-driven punishment, you feel guilty for being tough and maybe too tough. It feels like you can't win at these times!

Single parents also lack feedback and timely assistance. For them, no one is there to suggest a better way to discipline the child, no one is there to provide timely suggestions, no one is there to help them get a perspective, no one is there in times of emotional exhaustion to step in and take over, and no one is there to compliment them for their good work. As a single parent in one of our parent-training groups put it, "When I was heading for the cliff, no one was there to warn me that a dropoff was coming. I never knew I was going over the edge until I hit the bottom."

A Quick Fix.   The solution is obvious. Every single parent should go out and find Mr. or Ms. Right! If only it were that easy. After looking for a good spouse, many single parents have found some truth to an old joke:

Finding a good spouse is like looking for a parking space at the mall on the day after Thanksgiving. All the good ones are taken. And if a single parent jumps into a relationship that isn't right, he or she often makes matters worse.

Clearly, being a single parent fits into Category II. It cannot quickly be changed. In addition, some individuals choose to remain single. Single parents must take action so the stressor does not hamper their ability to parent. Part of the solution is to get more assistance.

Use Your Extended Family.   Single parents may find it necessary to ask their parents, siblings, aunts, uncles, and friends to routinely help with parenting responsibilities. When making this request, you should clearly explain the type of assistance that is needed, the times of the week that the assistance will be appreciated, and how long this help will be required. For example, Tom told his parents that he would like them to look after Sally two evenings a week, and to do that on a regular basis until Sally went back to school in the fall, which would be in two months.

Sometimes single parents live far away from their extended family. If you are in this situation and you are struggling to be a good caregiver, you might want to consider moving back home. Moving back home does not necessarily mean moving back in with Mom and Dad. It usually is sufficient just to move back to the home community, thereby affording access to your support network.

It is important that you understand that moving back home does not mean abandoning the aspirations, the goals, and the dreams that prompted moving away from home in the first place. Those aspirations, goals, and dreams are not dead. You simply put them on hold until you are better positioned and the child's behavior is back on track.

Develop a Support Group.   Of course, it might not be possible to enlist the help of your extended family. Maybe you don't have an extended family, or your extended family is unable for one reason or another to assist you. If this is the case, you need to find another way to develop a support group, which often means creating your own extended family. Based on the experience of the single parents seen in our clinic, developing a cooperative arrangement for child care is surprisingly easy. It starts by finding other single parents who are in a similar situation. Since there are so many divorces in this country, there are many people in your situation. Daycare centers are good places to look because they have a constant flow of parents dropping off and picking up children.

One single parent posted a note: MOTHER WOULD LIKE TO OCCASIONALLY TRADE CHILD CARE SERVICES. LET'S GET ACQUAINTED AND DISCUSS IT. MY PHONE NUMBER IS 555-2465.

This single parent got several responses to her posting. She ended up developing a close supportive relationship with another single mother. They not only shared child care, they became best friends who listened, affirmed, commiserated, and supported each other through thick and thin.

Cooperative arrangements for child care not only give single parents respite, but they often evolve into friendships. As friends, single parents invariably make time for coffee. Coffee therapy gives single parents a chance to vent, to get another perspective on issues and problems, to share thoughts and ideas about how to discipline, and to get validation for the parenting tasks they are doing well.

KEY CONCEPT

Single parents must either develop a support group or at least get additional assistance.

LOW-PAYING JOBS

Working at a low-paying job is another stressor frequently experienced by parents of defiant children.[18,19] Low-paying jobs can cause stress for three reasons. Low-paying jobs seldom provide health insurance, a retirement plan, or paid vacations. Second, low-paying jobs often lead to financial problems. Finally, low-paying jobs seldom give a person that all important sense of worth and importance.

I Am a Robot

Mrs. Simpson introduced herself to the parent-training group by saying, "I'm merely a cashier at a grocery store. It's a boring job. All I do is scan each item over the bar code reader. Then I look at the computer screen to see the total and ask for the money. As I give the customer her change, I say, 'Thank you for shopping at Miracle Mart.' Half of the customers don't even acknowledge my existence. They simply grab their groceries and walk out, making me feel like a faceless robot."

Self-Esteem.   Mrs. Simpson's self-esteem was being undermined by her job. But like others in our parent-training groups with low-paying jobs and working well below their ability, she found another avenue to meaningfully contribute to her community. She joined her church choir. A parent in a similar situation worked at the community food bank. Another was a library volunteer who read books to children every Saturday morning. Several fathers coached little league sports. Research supports the value of community involvement. People who contribute to the community have been shown to have a more positive outlook on life and to be happier overall.[20]

Financial.   Money problems are almost a synonym for a low-paying job. Money problems are such a common stressor for families that many community mental health centers and some civic-minded organizations offer financial counseling to low-income families either free or at a nominal cost. The financial counselor identifies dollars that are not being spent wisely, suggests mechanisms for consolidating loans that reduce interest payments, and helps the family develop and follow a budget. While the family does not have more money, better management of the family finances can lower the stress.

Even with good money management, some parents simply do not earn enough to make ends meet. The federal government, all states, and some communities offer assistance programs to low-income families. There is low-income housing, food stamps, Head Start for preschool children, and other services. The trick is to learn about the assistance system, and put it to work for you. Admittedly, it will not solve your financial problems. But it just might provide the help you need to get past this rough spot in the road.

Financial problems per se do not put children at risk for behavior problems. Rather, it is how the parents handle their financial problems that can negatively impact the children. Many couples do not calmly and privately discuss their financial problems. Instead, they allow their financial problems to fester until they burst out in unexpected ways at unfortunate times. If you find yourself in this situation, you must shelter your children from the emotional burden that typically accompanies financial problems. Nothing is accomplished when one parent derides the other in front of the children for wasteful spending, for not bringing home enough money, or for not paying pressing bills. Even calm, well-reasoned discussions about the family's financial problems should not be held within earshot of children. When children overhear such conversations, they tend to take unwarranted responsibility for the family's financial problems, often to the point of feeling guilty because they perceive themselves as one of the family's financial burdens.

CHILD STRESS

Parenting a child with any type of disability creates stress.[21] Parenting a defiant child is no exception.[22] Defiant children create stress by disrupting the household, skillfully pitting one parent against the other, and causing social embarrassment. Defiant children do not allow their parents to have predictable moments of peace. When the household is calm, the parents feel that they are walking on eggshells, waiting for the child's next temper tantrum. These tantrums have a way of coming at the worst possible moment. Take the child to a grocery store, and he has a tantrum in the checkout line. Bring the child to church, and she fights with other children in Sunday School. Have company over, and the child creates a scene.

Respite.   Parents who are raising a defiant child must routinely have time for themselves. This is not easy. It takes a good babysitter to manage a behaviorally challenged child. But that complication does not nullify the necessity. You not only deserve time for yourself, you need it in order to be an effective parent. If you don't make time for some fun and relaxation, you will find yourself resenting your child, which only makes matters worse.

KEY CONCEPT
Parents of a defiant child must have a break.

Fortunately, many community service organizations recognize this need. In our region of the country, Easter Seals provides respite to parents who are raising children with special needs, and some children with conduct problems qualify for their services, particularly if it is recommended by your family physician. There undoubtedly are other organizations around the county that also provide respite service.

CONCLUSION

The effectiveness of various treatments for defiant children and their families has been extensively investigated.[23] Among other findings, it has been determined that the child and the parents are most likely to benefit from treatment if the child's behavior is the only problem. The implication is clear. You must do everything possible to make the child's behavior the only problem. This means that you must make a plan for reducing Category I Stressors, and you must find a way so that Category II Stressors do not negatively impact your ability to be an effective parent.

APPLICATIONS

When parenting a child with behavior problems, there is no one big thing that you can do to solve the problem. Rather, the solution comes from doing a whole lot of little things, and doing them right. In the beginning, these little things may seem so removed from the heart of the problem that you might be tempted to skim over them or even skip doing them. Don't! Doing each of these "little" things will result, in the end, in a big difference.

In this book, the essential steps to helping your child are placed at the end of each chapter. These exercises, examples, and activities are linear and sequential. If you implement the applications at the end of each chapter, you will eventually see changes in your child's behavior.

This first chapter focused on your well-being, pointing out that it is essential that you identify your stressors and deal with them. Category I Stressors are those stressors that can be appreciably reduced, if not eliminated. Category II Stressors are those stressors that cannot quickly be reduced or eliminated. Since Category II Stressors can impact your ability to parent, they must be managed.

1. Check the stressors that are threatening your well-being or impairing your parenting ability.

    Category I Stressors: Can be reduced
    _____ Depression
    _____ Substance abuse
    _____ Isolation
    _____ Anxiety disorder
    _____ Marital discord
    _____ Other(s)

    Category II Stressors: Stressors whose impact on the child must be reduced
    _____ Single parenting
    _____ Low-paying job
    _____ Child's behavior
    _____ Financial problems

2. Category I Stressors can be significantly reduced. For example, Depression can be significantly reduced through treatment. Identify your top two Category I Stressors: _____ and _____

3. If a stressor is in Category I, some action is required to significantly reduce it. An example is given in the following table. Complete the table for your top two Category I Stressors.

Stressor	Action Steps	Time Line	Expected Outcome
Depression (example)	Make an appointment with physician	One week	Improved sleep, more energy, calmer emotions
Stressor 1: _____	_____	_____	_____
Stressor 2: _____	_____	_____	_____

4. Category II Stressors cannot be easily or quickly reduced, so a major effort is required so they do not negatively impact the child or appreciably diminish your ability to parent.

   Identify your top two Category II Stressors: _____ and _____

5. Complete the following table for your top two Category II
Stressors.

Stressor	Action Steps	Time Line	Expected Outcome
Finances (example)	Not discuss money problems in front of child	Immediate	Less stress on child
	Get financial counseling	Two weeks	Realistic budget, less conflict between parents
Stressor 1:			
Stressor 2:			

6. One stressor common to many parents of defiant children is
insufficient assistance and support. Do you need more support?
_____ Yes _____ No

If you checked yes, determine whether family, friends, or church, can
be a source of support to help reduce your stress level and to increase
your ability to provide high-quality parenting. By name, these people
or organizations are:

_____

_____

_____

_____

_____

_____

In the following table, consider each possible source and circle those that might be able to give you some assistance. Then read across the row, putting an X in each cell where you need assistance and these people might be able to provide that support.

Source	Time	Listening	Childcare	Money
Spouse				
Parents				
Grandparents				
Friends				
Siblings				
Aunts				
Uncles				
Others				

7. While all parents appreciate an occasional break from their children, parents who are raising defiant children must have scheduled breaks. You must have respite at least once a week. Don't wait for this respite to somehow happen. Plan it.

Look at the calendar for the next three weeks. Find at least one day each week that you are going to get a break from your parenting responsibilities and get out of the house. Don't make the mistake of thinking that "getting out" means spending money. It does not cost anything to go for a walk with a friend. It costs very little to meet your sister for a cup of coffee. Complete this chart for the next three weeks.

Activity	With Whom	Date, Time	Place	Cost

8. If it is desirable to secure additional support from a member of the family or extended family, it is useful to think about the support needed, the times when the support is needed, and for how long the support is needed. For every person in your potential support group, fill in the blanks on the following request:

_____ times per week for _____ please help me by _____.

9. Do you need to look beyond your immediate family or extended family for additional support? _____ Yes _____ No

If you checked yes, determine what assistance your church might offer or friends. You might also consider setting up a child care cooperative. What are the names of some people with whom you could set up a child care cooperative?

_____   _____

_____   _____

_____   _____

_____   _____

If you could not think of any people for your child care cooperative, the following note could be posted at your daycare center or, with appropriate permission, on the bulletin board in your church.

Parent would like to occasionally trade child care services. Let's get acquainted and discuss it. My telephone number is _____

2

Making the House a Home

A visitor to a house can immediately detect the climate of the home. Seeing that the house is neat and organized, the visitor concludes that the residents live together harmoniously and the household functions smoothly. If the house is chaotic, cluttered, and disorganized, the visitor suspects that the occupants are stressed.

Morning in the Smith Household

"Hurry up and get dressed," Mrs. Smith shouted at Megan, her 7-year-old daughter. "The school bus will be here any minute!"

"I can't find my shoe!" Megan yelled back from her bedroom. "Come help me!"

"Has anyone seen my book bag?" Sam called from the kitchen. "It was here last night, and now it's gone."

"The school bus is coming up the block," Mr. Smith warned. "You kids have 30 seconds to get out the bus stop. The driver won't sit there waiting for you."

"Here," Mrs. Smith said to Megan, handing her tennis shoes, "put these on."

"No! They don't go with my skirt," Megan screamed, running into the living room to look under the couch for her shoe. Sam hastily grabbed his book bag and ran for the bus. Five minutes later, Mrs. Smith found Megan's shoe. Since Megan had of course missed the bus, Mr. Smith had to take her to school, making him late for work.

Disorganized homes create stress and give defiant children fertile ground for sowing the seeds of chaos, confusion, and dysfunction. Therefore, creating a calm, smooth-operating home is critical to helping these children to better behavior.

> **KEY CONCEPT**
>
> Disorganized homes create stress and give defiant children fertile ground for planting the seeds of chaos and confusion.

ESTABLISH ORGANIZATION

The first place to start is with "things." Every "thing" in a home needs a place. This includes Dad's sporting equipment, Mom's shoes, and the children's toys. When every thing in the house is picked up, all of the things should be in specific places.

Admittedly, getting a house organized is hard and may even seem overwhelming. You may be asking, "Where do I find the time for this?" Sure, the initial organization of a house is work. But organizing the house has significant benefits, making the effort worth it. For starters, an organized house has a calming effect on every member of the household. This calming effect is particularly beneficial for children with behavior problems, who, by their very nature, tend to be unorganized and easily frustrated. These children bounce around a disorganized house doing things that irritate their siblings and their parents, creating conditions that demand reprimands and constant monitoring. When wondering whether you have time to organize your home, consider the adage: Pay me now, or pay me later. If you don't spend the time organizing the house to create the conditions that promote a calm, smooth-operating home, you will daily be reacting to the problems and stresses that go hand in hand with disorganization. Consider the Smith household. Wouldn't their day have started so much better if Megan knew where to find her shoes and Sam could find his book bag?

You can organize your house in a weekend. If the task seems overwhelming, recruit some help. Perhaps the children have an aunt or uncle, or a grandmother or grandfather, who likes to organize things. This one-time organization can be sold to the rest of the family as a big deal that will be celebrated by a special event, like everyone going out for a hot fudge sundae.

Once the commitment has been made to get the house organized and a plan has been made for doing it, here are some ideas that will help. You might want to reduce the amount of things that clutter the house. If there are more things than places to put them, some things have to be either discarded or put into storage. Also, get your child involved. In order to get your child to participate in the organization of her things, all people in the house need to organize their things. It must be a family project.

That begs the question, "Who goes first?" It seldom works for the parents to say to the child, "We need organization in this house. We'll start with your things." If the child is the first one selected to organize her things, she won't believe that everyone in the house is also going to comply. Furthermore, she will not have a model for how it will be done and how things will look once they are organized. A good place to start is with Dad's things. After all, in a child's eyes, Dad is the biggest strongest person in the house. If he has to organize his things, then the child probably has to organize his things. Everyone should be encouraged to help Dad organize his things. When children see that even Dad has to find a place for his things or discard them, they are less likely to feel put upon when it comes time for them to get organized.

The hardest things for children to organize are their toys. Toys should be put into one of two categories. There are outside toys, and there are inside toys. Outside toys are baseball bats, basketballs, tricycles, jumping ropes, soft balls, catching mitts, roller blades, and so on. If outside toys are played with inside the house, it is just a matter of time before a lamp gets knocked over, a wall gets dented, or the commotion gets on someone's nerves. To avoid this, outside toys go into a big box that sits next to the back door or in the garage. Outside toys should never be brought into the house.

With regard to inside toys, the same rule applies to them as to all "things"—the number of inside toys in the house cannot exceed the number of places to store them. If there are more toys than spaces, some toys must either be discarded or put into storage, such as a big box in the basement or in the garage. Since this rule has already been applied to Dad's sporting equipment and Mom's shoes, even a defiant child will understand that the rule also applies to him. That does not mean he will eagerly help organize his things, but it makes it likely that he will.

One of things that children balk at is discarding old toys that were once favorites, but haven't been used for months. If your child is reluctant to see anything "thrown away" there are two ways to jump that hurdle. The child might accept giving her things to Salvation Army, Goodwill, or a women's shelter with the explanation that needy children will enjoy them. If that fails to convince the child to part with the "thing," she can be told that her extra things do not have to be thrown out. They can be put into storage, such as in the basement or the attic. If such a space is not available, storage can be a big cardboard box that sits in a closet. Then the rule is that if your child wants something from storage, all she has to do is replace it with anything of comparable size.

No matter what you do or say, your child still might resist having her things organized. However, having set an example by organizing your things, you are in a position to say, "This rule applies to everyone in the house. There are no exceptions. If you do not help us, we will organize your things without you." If it comes to that, organize the child's things when she is asleep or out of the house so you can avoid a needless, emotion-laden battle.

It is critical that after you organize the house, the entire family sits down to discuss the rules for keeping the house in order. These words work, "We just organized the house. Now, we will be able to find things when we need them. But we need to keep the house organized." Turning toward the children, ask, "Does anyone have any ideas about how we can keep the house organized?" With guidance, the family will develop rules that cover these basic points:

- Outside toys are for playing outside.
- Every "thing" has a specific place.

- If some "thing" comes out of storage, something of comparable size must replace it.
- Each evening, everything in the house is put in its place for the night.
- Everyone helps with the evening pickup, contributing at his or her ability level.

> **KEY CONCEPT**
>
> Things in the house need to have a place. When each day is over, everything needs to put away in its place.

When children help around the house, they learn two valuable lessons. The first valuable lesson is that in a harmonious household, everyone has responsibilities. The second valuable lesson is that organization makes the house calmer and less chaotic. Furthermore, organization skills and habits serve children well in school and in life.

There are little tricks that make it easier for your child to help keep the house organized. For preschool children, it is useful to use a black marker to outline the shape of the thing as it sits in its storage space. If you do not want the mark to be permanent, trace the shape onto a piece of paper that is laid or taped in the drawer. Storage boxes are also useful, and they don't have to be fancy or cost money. Shoeboxes work great for holding crayons and pencils. Another shoebox can hold plastic action figures, and a third shoebox can hold legos. A picture or sketch on the box helps the child remember what goes in the box. Older children like colored plastic crates that can be stacked or plastic containers that can be stored under their bed.

PLAN THE DAY

Failure to plan is planning to fail. That certainly describes a day in the life of a parent who is raising a behaviorally challenged child. If the supervising parent starts the day without a plan for the child's activities, many of his activities will end in disaster. For example, a neighborhood friend comes over to play. The child and her friend might play together just fine for thirty minutes and maybe (but not likely) an hour. But if this playtime had not been thought out, it will almost assuredly end in a squabble or a fight. The parent then sends the friend home and reprimands his child.

This is a terrible outcome. It is terrible because every time parents reprimand their child, they are straining the parent–child relationship. That terrible outcome could have been avoided with just a little planning. Before
your child's friend comes over to play, ask yourself, "How long can these
two children play together without getting in a squabble? Thirty minutes."
Then both children should be told that the playtime will be thirty minutes.
You should also ask yourself, "What activities are the children most likely
to play together harmoniously? And how long will each activity hold their
interest?" This preplanning takes only a few minutes, and it means the difference between setting your child up to fail versus setting your child up to
be successful. You set your child up for success by reducing the child's
opportunities for engaging in unacceptable behavior and increasing the
chances that each activity ends on a good note. This may seem like a small
issue, but a child's day is comprised of small issues. When a succession of
"small" issues go well, the child feels good about herself. Planning, meaning giving a little thought to how the day will go, helps children be successful with the succession of small issues that comprise their day.

> **KEY CONCEPT**
>
> A well-organized, smooth-functioning home establishes the
> structure children need in order to behave appropriately.

A plan does not have to be written out as a schedule. It can be in your
head. After all, the purpose of a plan for the day is merely to lay out the
time and sequence of what activities probably will happen that day and
think about the structure, the materials, and the support the defiant child
needs so that those activities to go smoothly. Remember, younger children
have short attention spans. It is unrealistic to plan for 4-year-old children
to play in the sandbox for an hour. If such a time block was planned, it is
all but guaranteed that after fifteen minutes the children will lose interest
and start to do unacceptable things, like throw sand at a playmate.

Take into consideration your child's natural biological rhythm. For
example, if your child takes a nap at 2:30 p.m., at 2:00 he should do a
quiet activity, slowing him down and preparing him to rest. After the nap,
he probably wants to be active. So playing in the wading pool would be a

better activity after nap time than listening to a book tape. Finally, the plan should include at least one time each day when you participate in an activity with your child so that you can use this interaction time to strengthen your relationship with the child.

Having a plan in mind for the day also helps you prepare for the child's activities. For example, if playing in the wading pool is on the agenda, you increase the likelihood of moving smoothly from the just-concluded activity to the wading pool by laying out the swimming suits and towels in advance. If the swimming suits and towels are not laid out, it is unlikely that young children, especially those with short attention spans and limited impulse control, will patiently wait while you get those items.

Sample Morning Plan for a 6-Year-Old Girl on a Nonschool Day

08:00	Family eats breakfast
08:15	Quiet time, play with toys
08:45	Get dressed, brush teeth, and comb hair
09:00	Accompany parent on trip to the grocery store
10:30	Morning snack
11:00	Watch DVD
12:00	Put plates and cups on the kitchen table
12:10	Family eats lunch

There is nothing hard and fast about a plan. The purpose of a plan is simply to prompt you to give some advance thought about what will make the day unfold best for your child. Without a plan, parents have a strong tendency to follow the adage: Let sleeping dogs lie. That adage might work with dogs, but it does not work with behaviorally challenged children. Left without structure and direction, these children are bound to do something wrong. It is only a matter of time. If a child with behavior problems spends too much time in unstructured play, that play invariably ends in a behavioral wreck. If he is playing with a friend or a sibling, the play degenerates into a squabble. If he is playing alone, the play eventually morphs into some destructive action, like coloring in the coloring book evolving into coloring on the wall. Then it goes from bad to worse. Because when children are caught doing something wrong, the supervising adult has to intervene. But defiant children get angry when reprimanded or redirected, after becoming noncompliant and combative. Suddenly, a small seemingly insignificant issue grows into a catastrophe, ruining everyone's day.

Many children with behavior problems have a difficult time getting from the end of one activity to the beginning of the next one. These transitions can be managed with a few tricks. You can help your child make the transition successfully if the activity that is just concluding has a clear "finish." If the activity has a clear finish, it is obvious to everyone, especially to the child, that the activity is completed and over with. For example, putting together a 25-piece puzzle has a clear finish. The puzzle is finished when all 25 pieces have been put into the puzzle. Snack time also has a clear finish. A snack is finished when the food on the plate has been eaten. However, many activities do not have a clear finish. What is the "finish" for playing in the sandbox? Or what is the "finish" for playing with legos? Activities that do not have an obvious finish need something to mark the end of the activity.

With most children, a parent can say, "That's enough time in the sandbox. It is time to play on the swing set." However, that approach does not work for defiant children. Defiant children do not like being told what to do. Giving them a verbal directive is like waving a red flag at a fighting bull.

> **KEY CONCEPT**
> Defiant children do not like being told what to do.

In lieu of telling a defiant child what to do, it works best to communicate your expectations using some nonverbal means. In this sandbox situation, you could use a kitchen timer to signal the end. The nice thing about a kitchen timer is that when the time is up, it has an irritating and obvious ring. It just feels good to stop doing what one is doing and push that button that stops the ringing. When using a timer to signal the finish of an activity, estimate how long your child will remain engaged in that activity, and then set the timer for a little less time. The next "trick" is to give your defiant child a sense of control. To do that, you ask, "Would you like to set the timer?" If he indicates an interest, say, "Push 1 and then push 5. Good! You set the time for 15 minutes. When the timer goes off, it will be time to come in." Done in this manner, when the timer rings, the child is responding to the "finish" that he set. He has control!

The bell rings on the timer. Without saying anything, the parent comes over to the sandbox and holds out the timer, motioning for the child to push the button that stops the beeping. When the child does this, the parent gives an approving head nod. Then the parent walks with the child into the house,

A plan for the day is flexible. If you had intended that the child would play in the sandbox in the afternoon but it starts to rain, you quickly redo the plan. After all, the plan that you mentally laid out at the beginning of the day does not dictate. The plan is your guide for helping the children's day go smoothly, nothing more.

FAMILY TIME

It is important that each day there are activities that draw the entire family together. Eating meals together is particularly important. But just eating together is not sufficient. While eating together, the family members need to talk to each other. To facilitate talking and listening, turn off the television and any other distracting background noise.

Eating supper together as a family is important. It is one time of the day when everyone is together as a family. When the members of the family talk to each other and listen, it brings them closer together. In addition, it gives children an opportunity to listen to adults and learn about that larger world that they are slowly entering. So it is no wonder that families who routinely eat their meals together raise preschool children who acquire better language skills.[24] When families eat together, their elementary-aged children improve their grades and do better on nationwide achievement tests.[25] Most important, when families eat together, the children are also better adjusted and behaved[26]—something that is particularly important for children who are having behavior problems.

QUIET TIME

Defiant children often spin out of control as the day goes on. They wind themselves up, but have no ability to slow down. They just keep going at an increasingly frenetic pace until they are emotionally exhausted. Reaching that point, they have an outburst or a temper tantrum.

To avoid this outcome, there should be one or two quiet times during the day for children. A quiet time allows them to recharge their batteries, giving them the capacity to continue controlling and self-monitoring their behavior. After a quiet time, these children behave much better. A scheduled quiet time has one other advantage. A quiet time gives you a respite during the day.

REDUCE THE EXPOSURE TO VIOLENCE

Children who are noncompliant and defiant are usually also aggressive. Unfortunately, in the world in which we live, children are exposed to aggression almost every place they look. In particular, children see a great deal of aggression and violence on television, in the movies, and even on the games that are marketed expressly for them.

Our culture glorifies aggression and violence. Turn on the television at any time of the day and chances are someone is being killed, beaten, or tormented. Saturday morning television cartoons show courageous soldiers fighting ugly aliens from faraway planets, valiant knights slaying mean warriors from the evil empire, and good cops shooting bad guys. Even such seemingly benign cartoons such as *Road Runner* portray violent acts, like Wile E. Coyote getting revenge by rolling a boulder off a cliff onto the beeping bird. Violence is so prevalent on television that it has been estimated that by the age of 14 the average child has witnessed 11,000 murders.[27]

The affect of television violence on children was once debated, but that discussion is over. Watching violence promotes aggression. The first evidence was provided way back in 1961. In a now classic study, Albert Bandura, a psychologist at Stanford University, had a group of preschool children play with a large inflatable doll.[28] The children did so without displaying aggression toward the doll. Bandura also had a different group of preschool children observe an adult exuberantly hit, kick, punch, and throw the large inflatable doll. When the adult left the room, this group of preschoolers proceeded to display the same acts of aggression toward the doll that the adult had just modeled.

Bandura's study begged an interesting question. What happens when children watch the violence on television? Does watching people model aggression on television cause children to be more aggressive? Leonard Eron, then a professor at the University of Chicago, explored the answer to this question by surveying parents about the amount of time their children watched television and the types of television programs they viewed.[29] Eron also had the children's peers rate each child's level of aggression. He found that the more violence that boys watched on television, the more aggressively they played with other children.

However, not everyone was convinced by these laboratory studies.[30] In Bandura's study, children saw a strange man doing strange things in a strange situation—hardly a typical childhood experience. Eron merely surveyed parents as to what they thought their children were watching on television. Sure the television was on, but who knows if the children were actually watching it?

To obtain a definitive answer as to whether watching violence on television causes children to become more aggressive, scientists went into the real world.[31] In one such study, researchers discovered that plans were underway to bring television to a small isolated community in Northern Canada. Knowing this, the researchers went to this isolated community, which they dubbed Notel, and measured the children's aggression a year before television arrived.[32] Two years after television arrived, the scientists returned to the community to assess the level of the children's aggression. They found that after television was brought to the community, the physical violence among the children increased 160 percent. Other real-world research found that the amount and type of violence that children view on television predicts the amount of aggression they display as young adults.[33]

> **KEY CONCEPT**
>
> Children who watch violence on television are more aggressive.

The implications are clear. Children who watch violence and aggression on television tend to use aggression to solve their disputes with other children and to get what they want from their parents. If you are concerned about the amount of aggression that your child is displaying, you must actively monitor the television programs your child is watching. In order to provide the necessary supervision, your children should not have a television set in their bedroom, downstairs in a playroom, or any other place in the house where you cannot readily monitor what they are watching. The television programs should be selected to prevent children from watching programs with violent content.

Also, TV watching should be a planned activity incorporated into the child's day in small doses. There is another equally important reason to limit the amount of television that children watch. When children are being "entertained" by watching television, they are not playing and interacting with friends or adults. They are missing interactions are essential for them to learn how to get along with others. Furthermore, watching television detracts from doing activities that help children develop important visual–motor skills and it arrests their overall physical development.

> **KEY CONCEPT**
>
> Parents must monitor the television programs that their children watch.

Our society glorifies violence in other ways. Many of the video and DVD games marketed for children teach them that it is okay for "good" people to use aggression against "bad" people. After playing such games, children begin to believe that that everyone respects and admires tough aggressive people who stand up for their rights. Some DVD games even construct virtual worlds wherein children are invited to become perpetrators of violence. Children who are displaying disturbing levels of aggressive should not be entering a virtual world that encourages violence, nor should they be shooting at people with plastic guns, hitting other children with oversized boxing gloves, or playing with any other toy that encourages them to "pretend" to be aggressive.

> **KEY CONCEPT**
>
> The home should be as free as possible from all things that glorify and encourage violence and aggression.

CREATE A CLIMATE OF VALUING

Home is a place for children to be valued and affirmed. Such valuing and affirmation is the best antidote for children's outbursts of noncompliance and defiance. Valuing children is powerful. The power of valuing children was demonstrated in the book *400 Losers*.[34] In that book, Ahlstrom and Havighurst, professors of education at the University of Chicago, told about an extensive experiment with 400 high-risk, inner-city adolescents in Kansas. Starting in the eighth grade, half of the 400 high-risk adolescents were randomly selected to continue their traditional public education. The other half of the students were enrolled in a five-year program that was considered to be an excellent program for high-risk youth. These 200 students had small class sizes and individual tutoring. Their classroom education was integrated into training on work habits and occupational skills. As the students advanced in school, they were paid increasingly higher wages as they progressed from work training to full-time employment. What could be better? Understandably, the researchers expected that these 200 students who got this excellent education would be successful.

When the students in the study all turned 18, the researchers checked on the status of each one. They expected that the 200 students who participated in the elaborate educational programming would be far more successful than the 200 students who received traditional public education. They weren't. Nearly all of the 400 high-risk youth were failing. Few of them were continuing their education or training. Instead, they either were in trouble with the law, they were unemployed, they were using drugs, or they were gang members. This poor outcome happened to the 200 students who received the traditional education, and it also happened to the 200 students who received the extensive and expensive five-year-long intervention services.

However, in looking over the data, the researchers made a surprising discovery. They found that some of the 400 high-risk adolescents made it. One year after high school, a small number of students from both the traditional education group and the excellent education group either had a job or they were continuing their education and training. Furthermore, none of this small group of students had been arrested for any crime. They were successful!

What was it that allowed these precious few high-risk students to escape what seemed to be their predetermined fate? The researchers discovered that there was one factor that made the difference between the high-risk students who failed and high-risk students who found success. The factor that made the difference was being valued. The students who were successful had found an adult who valued them, who believed in them, and, when necessary, was there for them.

The power of valuing children is captured by this poem by an unknown author.

> "I got two A's," the small boy said,
> His voice filled with glee.
> His father very bluntly asked,
> "Why didn't you get three?"
>
> "Mom, I've got the dishes done,"
> The girl called from the door.
> Her mother very calmly said,
> "Did you sweep the floor?"
>
> "I mowed the grass," the tall boy said,
> "And put the mower away,"
> His father asked him with a shrug,
> "Did you clean off the clay?"
>
> The children in the house next door
> Seemed happy and content.
> The same things happened over there,
> But this is how it went.
>
> "I got two A's," the small boy said,
> His voice filled with glee.
> His father proudly said, "That's great;
> I'm glad you belong to me."
>
> "Mom, I've got the dishes done,"
> The girl called from the door.
> Her mother smiled and softly said,
> "Each day I love you more."
>
> "I've mowed the grass," the tall boy said,
> "and put the mower away."
> His father answered with much joy,
> "You've made my happy day."

Children deserve a little praise
For tasks they're asked to do,
If they're to lead a happy life,
So much depends on you.

A HABIT OF VALUING

Valuing your child is important. Valuing and affirming your child is far too important to be left to chance and happenstance. If you want your child to overcome his behavior problems, you must daily value your child.

"But what if my child never does anything right?" some parents in our parent-training groups ask. The question is understandable. Many defiant children never make it from one hour to the next without doing something wrong, especially when we compare them to what is expected. The answer is to lower the bar. All children do SOMETHING right, even if is just getting out bed in the morning. Don't wait for your child to rise to meet your expectations before you value her. Lower your expectations. Find things that your child is doing right, and value those little things.

Also, develop rituals for valuing your child at special accomplishments and at important milestones. For example, you put a YOU DID IT poster on the refrigerator door when your child kicks the game-winning goal in soccer match. Acknowledge and celebrate his major developmental milestones by helping him call a grandparent to share the good news. Do something special to celebrate the first day she walks, the first day she talks, and the first day she goes to kindergarten. Put the remembrances of these celebrations in his scrapbook, which he can (and will) look at from time to time as he grows and matures. When she goes to school, put the art work that she brings home and the perfect spelling test on the refrigerator door. At the supper table that evening, tell the rest of the family of the child's accomplishment.

One family tried to have a discussion every night about things that they were thankful for that happened during the day. It was a small thing, but it gave the kids a chance to focus on the positive, and it gave the parents a natural moment to tell the kids they were proud or touched by something they did that day, even if it was something small like they held the door open for someone or remembered to wash their hands before dinner. A child who feels valued and affirmed learns that he likes basking in that warm light, and he looks for things that he can do that will please you and bring him even more recognition and affirmation.

> **KEY CONCEPT**
>
> Valuing children is the secret for helping children with challenging behaviors.

APPLICATIONS

It is necessary to create a calm, well-organized living environment that by its rhythm eases stress, promotes tranquility, encourages children's best efforts, and prompts parents to praise liberally.

1. Organizing the home:

> Is organization a problem in your home?
> ___ Yes ___ No

If you checked yes, have each person in the home organize his or her things, starting with the oldest person in the house and working downward by age.

You may need containers. Boxes that once held reams of paper are great for long-term storage since they have easily removable lids and can be labeled. You may be able to get these at a local school for free. Plastic baskets and plastic crates work well for children's rooms where items are used regularly. Laundry hampers in each child's bedroom keep clothes off the floor. Bookshelves and toy boxes can also significantly reduce clutter.

The entire family should be involved in the organizational task. When finished, every item in the house should have a storage or resting place. Outside toys and equipment should remain outside.

After this big organization, there should be a family meeting where a plan is jointly developed and discussed to set a family pickup time each day. Be sure to keep the assignments and expectations age appropriate.

2. Structuring the home:

> Do the major daily activities in your home, such as meals, playtime, naps, and bedtime, happen according to a plan?
> ____ Yes ___ No

If you checked no, think through a plan that you can implement tomorrow. Although it takes extra time, it will help your defiant child if you can post the plan on the refrigerator or on another clearly visible place. Be sure that the plan contains a time that you can participate with your child in a fun, child-centered activity.

As you think through the plan, consider how you can be prepared for the activities. For example, if you and your child plan to bake some cookies, you will want to make sure you have the necessary ingredients since impulsive and defiant children have a hard time waiting to search for supplies and an even harder time if a planned fun activity needs to be cancelled.

Use the chart on pages 48–50 chart as a guide for thinking through a plan for a child for the first few hours of the day.

3. Dealing with the culture of violence as it invades your home:

> Does your child watch television programs, cartoons, or videos that expose him or her to violence?
> ___ Yes ___ No

If you checked yes, set a goal to significantly reduce your child's exposure to violence within the next thirty days. A good place to start is with an inventory of the toys, games, television shows, videos, and books that bring violence into your home.

Toys _____

Games _____

Television Shows _____

Videos _____

Books _____

If some violence-promoting items are taken away, you will want to replace them with an appropriate alternative activity. Some suggestions are listed below. These suggestions come from common websites such as barnesandnoble.com and Amazon.com. There is a short description of each item on the website, which can give you ideas as to how they can be used with your child. Defiant children are lacking in social skills. Books, CDs, and DVDs are tools that you can use to help your child begin to understand how others solve problems and deal with challenges in positive ways. You can use the material as a forum for discussion of character, values, and behavior in a non-threatening and thought-provoking way. This list is meant to get you started. You can continue to check for new materials by using search words such as "self- esteem," "problem solving," "decision making," "social skills," "peer pressure," "overcoming diversity," or "making friends."

Children Ages 4–7
Books

I Knew You Could!: A Book for All the Stops in Your Life, by Craig Dortman, Christina Ong (Illustrator), and Watty Piper. ISBN: 0448431483 $9.59

I'm Gonna Like Me: Letting Off a Little Self-Esteem, by Jamie Lee Curtis and Laura Cornell (Illustrator). ISBN: 0060287616 $11.89

I Like Myself! by Karen Beaumont and David Catrow (Illustrator). ISBN: 0152020136 $12.80

It's Hard to Be Five: *Learning How to Work My Control Panel*, by Jamie Lee Curtis and Laura Cornell (Illustrator). ISBN: 0060080957 $11.89

CDs

You Sing a Song and I'll Sing a Song, book and read-along audio, $16.98

Quiet Time $13.48

Free to Be You and Me, book and read-along audio, $9.58

DVDs

Shrek 2 $19.98

Finding Nemo $23.98

Mary Poppins $23.98

Children Ages 8–11
Books

Tales of a Fourth Grade Nothing, by Judy Blume. ISBN: 0142401013 $5.99

How to Eat Fried Worms, by Thomas Rockwell. ISBN: 0440421853 $5.99

The Roald Dahl Treasury, by Roald Dahl. ISBN: 067001663 $10.30

Jackie Robinson: Strong Inside and Out (TFK Biographies Series). ISBN: 0060576006 $3.99

True Stories: Girls Inspiring Stories of Courage and Heart (American Girl Library Series). ISBN: 1584857447 $7.95

Helen Keller: A Photographic Story of a Life (DK Biography Series). ISBN: 0756603390 $4.99

CDs

American Idol Greatest Moments $13.98

The BFG, by Roald Dahl, audio book, $16.35

Amelia Bedelia, by Peggy Parish, book and read-along audio, $9.99

Little House on the Prairie, by Laura Ingalls Wilder, audio book, $17.13

Island of the Blue Dolphins, by Scott O'Dell, audio book, $13.57

Disney Cars: Read-Along $7.99

4. Make a list of the alternative toys, games, videos, and books that would interest your child. Share your list with friends and relatives who might be buying your children birthday or holiday gifts.

5. Move the TV and the computer out of the child's bedroom and into a place where what is being viewed can readily be monitored. Consider getting a V-chip that blocks out unwanted television programs.

6. Creating a positive atmosphere in the home: Is there a need to increase the ways your home reflects pride in its occupants and nurtures their development?

      ___ Yes ___ No

If you checked yes, consider adding the following:

- An area for inspirational poems or posters

- A place to display the children's good work, usually the refrigerator door

- A place to display the child's hobbies, collections, or projects

- A time, such as dinner or bedtime, to recognize and celebrate accomplishments

TIME	ACTIVITY	NEEDED MATERIALS	HOW THIS WILL HELP A DEFIANT CHILD
07:00	Child wakes up		
07:30	Breakfast	Set table and have in mind what will be offered. For example, cereal boxes and bowls are placed on the table the night before.	Defiant children are prone to arguing over what they eat or don't eat. If there are a few choices, such as two kinds of cereal boxes on the table, defiant children will more likely choose one and begin eating.
07:45	Individual activity box with play objects such as blocks, cars, puzzles while the parents get the family going	An activity box that contains a few high-interest items. Frequently change a few items in the box so it maintains interest.	Defiant children have a hard time behaving during transitions, such as from breakfast to entertaining themselves for a while with an appropriate activity. When parents are busy with demands such as getting themselves or family members ready for the day, this "down time" is fertile ground for them to demand attention by misbehaving. A box of fun activities provides the transition from breakfast to independent play and gives your child a chance to make a good activity choice.

08:00	Parent facilitates grooming activities	Set out clothes and toothbrush with your child the previous night.	Defiant children are prone to argue over what to wear. By giving your child ample time before bed to set out what she wants to wear the next day, there is a greater chance that your child will willingly and quickly get dressed without delaying the family.
08:10	Exercise activity like going for a walk with a parent or riding a tricycle		Defiant and impulsive children are usually full of energy in the morning. By planning a physical activity you can take advantage of that energy to provide your child with an appropriate outlet.
08:45	Child helps with parent's errands such as going grocery shopping, going to the bank or dry cleaners		Children learn appropriate ways to interact with others by watching their parents. Defiant children often lack the ability to read social cues. Letting your child watch you as you interact with others and talking about your interactions will help defiant children learn social skills.

(cont.)

TIME	ACTIVITY	NEEDED MATERIALS	HOW THIS WILL HELP A DEFIANT CHILD
09:45	Snack	Snack items	Defiant and impulsive children have a harder time behaving as they get hungry (or tired). Plan for this by keeping small, healthy snacks available and offering them before signs of crankiness appear.
10:00	Quiet time such as listening to a parent read or listening to a book on tape		Quiet time allows a defiant, aggressive, and impulsive child to relax and decrease agitation resulting from interactions that have not gone well. Without a calming time, defiant children's misbehavior will likely escalate.

3

Strengthening the Parent–Child Relationship

A Game for Losers

Maria knew that she and her son Justin did not have a strong relationship. Wanting to strengthen their relationship, she decided to play a game with Justin. So one rainy Sunday afternoon, she said, "Justin, let's play a board game. What shall we play?"

"Trouble!" Justin enthusiastically replied. "I never lose." Wanting him to win, Maria gave Justin the first roll of the dice. He started in the lead and maintained the lead for the first five minutes of the game. However, his mother gradually edged closer. On the next roll of the dice, Maria came up with a four and a two. "Six," Justin said, proudly proclaiming his ability to quickly add the numbers. "One, two, three . . . " he counted, putting his finger on each square as he marched toward the spot where his mother's marker would land. Reaching six, Justin found his finger on the same square that his marker occupied. According to the rules of the game, this meant that Justin had to move his marker back to the start box. Seeing that, Justin flipped the board over and stormed off.

"It's okay, Justin," Maria called after him. "I won't make you go back to the beginning." But Justin was not listening. Dejectedly, Maria put the game away. "How," she wondered, "can I build a relationship with my son when he blows up over the least little thing?"

Justin is like most of the defiant children we see in our clinical practice. They do not have a close relationship with their parents. But developing a close relationship is crucial to improving a defiant child's behavior. But how, you might be wondering, does the parent–child relationship develop?

A CLOSE RELATIONSHIP BEGINS WITH ATTACHMENT

In 1958 John Bowlby, a British developmental psychologist, published the first in a series of publications that stretched over four decades about a phenomenon that he called Attachment Theory.[35,36] Like others before him, Bowlby noted that during infants' first six months, they increasingly do things to bring people within closer proximity. For example, when infants see someone, they make gestures and noises intended to draw that person closer, possibly resulting in being picked up, cuddled, and maybe even fed. During the second six months, these proximity and interaction-promoting behaviors begin to be integrated into a coherent system. According to Bowlby, it is at this stage that attachment begins to form.[37] Attachment can be seen in the differential way infants respond to strangers as opposed to a caregiver. When infants see strangers, they stare wide eyed at them, often lying motionless as if to avoid being spotted. In contrast, when infants see a caregiver, they coo and smile, inviting interaction. They are attached.

Most infants form strong attachments to a caregiver, usually their mother. This strong bond develops when the caregiver understands the infant's signals and responds appropriately and consistently. However, sometimes the caregiver and the infant don't become strongly bonded. This can happen for two reasons.

A strong attachment does not develop if the caregiver is unwilling or unable to respond to the infant's signals. Also, a strong attachment does not develop if the caregiver cannot read the infant's signals. This latter situation is particularly likely to happen in the case of defiant children who were born with a difficult temperament. Such was the case for Mrs. Baker.

An Inconsolable Infant

"When my son Erik was a newborn," Mrs. Baker related during a parent-training group, "he was irritable and hard to console. In fact, Erik was so fussy that the doctor kept us in the hospital a couple of extra days just to see if something was wrong with him. There wasn't. He just liked to cry and fuss. Erik fussed whatever I did. If he was wet, he fussed. When I changed him, he still fussed. If he was hungry, he fussed. When I fed him, he continued to fuss. Even when I picked him up and cuddled him, he fussed. Erik fussed regardless of what I did. Pretty soon it was just easier to let him fuss."

Mrs. Baker's response to Erik is understandable. Infant–parent interactions are a two-way street. In order for parent–child bonding to occur, the parent has to respond positively to the child's signals, but the child must also show that she finds the caregiver's attention soothing and comforting. When an infant does not respond positively to the parent's attempts to be nurturing and affectionate, the parent may eventually stop trying.

A strong parent–child bond is critical to the child's later social development. Mary Ainsworth, working at John Hopkins University, used a procedure called the Stranger Situation to study how the strength of the parent–infant bond affects children when they become toddlers.[38] Ainsworth had mothers place their toddlers in an unfamiliar playroom where there was a stranger, and then leave. After a period of absence, the mother re-entered the playroom. Toddlers who, as infants, had formed a strong bond with their mothers, immediately approached their mothers, initiating physical contact and interaction. However, toddlers who, as infants, had not formed a strong bond with their mothers vacillated between being angry at their mothers and seeking physical contact and reassurance. Some of the toddlers actually snubbed and ignored their mothers upon their re-entry.

Moving up the age scale, researchers subsequently found that the 12- and 18-month-old toddlers who resisted and shunned their mothers in the Stranger Situation went on to display behavior problems in preschool.[39] As preschoolers, these children were unfeeling and defiant [40, 41]

The research shows that the infant–parent bonding laid down during a newborn's first six months provides the foundation upon which the evolving parent–child relationship is built. As previously mentioned, this is borne out in our clinical experience. The defiant children that we see do not have a close relationship. Indeed, they seem to be on edge, looking for a reason to be noncompliant.

Bowlby's Attachment Theory and the subsequent research explain how a weak bond develops between defiant children and their parents. But that all happened in the past. And the past is just that. It is the past. It cannot be relived. Today, the only relevant question is whether now, at this point in your child's development, can you still develop a positive relationship with your child? The answer is yes. Children are resilient. The bond between you and your defiant child can be markedly strengthened. Furthermore, as has been stated, strengthening the parent–child bond is the key to helping children to stop being defiant.

A BANK ACCOUNT ANALOGY

A positive parent–child relationship can be compared to having money in an account at your child's bank. Your account in the child's bank operates like this: Every time you value your child by making a positive comment or praising a specific action, you put money into your account. But every time you reprimand your child, even if the reprimand is warranted, you take money out of your account. A reprimand draws more money out of your account than a positive remark puts into the account. To keep money in the account, you must do a lot more valuing than reprimanding.

When you give your child a directive, the child immediately checks the amount of valuing dollars that you have in your account. If you have money in your account, the child generally obeys the request. But if your account is running a deficit, the child seldom complies.

Children are good bankers. They tally every transaction, and at their bank there are no free services. When you reprimand, make too many demands, praise too little, and value too seldom, your account becomes overdrawn. When your account is overdrawn, your child becomes non-compliant and defiant.

Unfortunately, once children become defiant it is hard for parents to then develop a strong relationship with them. It is difficult for two reasons. One reason is that defiant children lack essential relationship-building skills. Maria certainly experienced her son's skill deficit when they tried to play Trouble. Justin could not handle losing.

It is also difficult to develop a strong parent–child bond because defiant children actively resist it. Such children work at keeping their parents at an emotional distance because, in their eyes, relationships are all about control. Defiant children will not tolerate being controlled! Therefore, they keep adults, even their parents, at an emotional distance.

Defiance and attachment are opposite sides of the same coin. So the best way to decrease your child's noncompliance and defiance is to strengthen the parent–child relationship.

THE ESSENTIAL RELATIONSHIP SKILLS

Based on our experience of providing a clinic for children with behavior problems and their parents, defiant children are missing all, or at least most, of five essential relationship skills. The five essential relationship skills that defiant children must learn are these:

- Allowing an adult to label their behavior without becoming defensive.
- Appreciating an adult's praise.
- Allowing an adult to participate in jointly doing a task.
- Taking turns at an activity.
- Understanding that a competitive game is about friendship, not winning or losing.

> **KEY CONCEPT**
>
> Defiant children must be taught how to participate in nurturing relationships.

TEACHING THE FIVE RELATIONSHIP SKILLS

The skills that your child needs to learn depends on your child's age and whether a skill that should be present at that age is missing. These skills are acquired sequentially. They build on each other. Much like using bricks to build a house, you have to start at the foundation and work up. The first essential relationship skill that your child must learn is to allow you to label his or her behavior.

ACCEPTING LABELING

Most 2-year-old children accept having their behavior labeled. For example, Sally, a 3-year-old girl with no significant behavior problems, smiles when her dad says, "Sally, you are putting on your shoes." In contrast, most defiant children do not accept having their behavior labeled. When Donald's dad said, "Donald, you are playing with your fire truck," Donald gave the fire truck a hard push across the floor and stomped out of the room. Defiant children do not like it when their parents label their behavior. They do not like having their behavior labeled because it implies that they are listening to what their parent is saying. And if they appear to be listening to what their parent says, it also appears like they are complying with what the parent says. Defiant children do not like to comply because compliance implies control.

You can easily tell whether your child will accept having his behavior labeled. Just label something your child is doing and see how he reacts. If he stops doing the activity, if the muscles in his forearm tense, if his jaw tightens, if his face flushes red or blanches white, he does not like it when you label his actions. He might even throw the activity, tear it up, or scream at you to go away. Or he might simply stop doing the activity. If he has any of those reactions, you must teach him how to accept having his behavior labeled.

Defiant children are taught in gradual increments to accept having their behavior labeled. The first step is simply to notice what your child is doing, and to let her know that you are noticing. To do this, when your child is engaging in an appropriate behavior, you acknowledge that you have noticed what your child is doing. For example, you say, "You are combing your doll's hair." This comment sounds harmless and unobtrusive to you. But if your child is missing this relationship-building skill, she will react negatively. If she does, you must notice even her smallest indicator of resistance. Seeing her resistance, it is critical that you mask your natural and understandable tendency to be offended. However, hiding those reactions is incredibly difficult. It takes practice. When your child flashes signs that she did not like to have her actions labeled, you must not raise an eyebrow. You must not frown. You must not pull back even slightly. If you do, your child will immediately detect your subtle signs of disapproval, and she will act out.

Start with labeling just one appropriate behavior at a time. The first few times that you label an appropriate behavior, expect your child to react adversely. When you see that your child is becoming slightly irritated by the labeling, do not say a thing or even move an eyebrow. Wait. Your child probably will go back to doing the activity. However, if she does not re-engage within a few seconds and continues to flash indications that she is upset, walk away and give her space.

At this beginning stage of relationship building, you must not intersperse labeling with giving advice, providing guidance, offering help, or praising. If you were to point at a puzzle piece and say, "There is the cloud you need for the top of your puzzle," your child is more apt to throw the puzzle piece at you than to accept your assistance.

Getting your child to accept having her behavior labeled is a slow gradual process—often a painfully slow process. When done best, you appear to casually notice what your child is doing, describe it as if musing out loud, and move on.

The final step in helping your child have her behavior labeled is to gradually decrease the distance between you and your child as you observe and label her actions. Eventually, you should be able to sit right beside your child and label a behavior without seeing any indication of distress or resentment. In fact, you will see your child smile and maybe even do the action with more intent and purpose.

Labeling is surprisingly hard. To effectively teach your child this relationship-building skill you must:

- Label only one behavior at a time. Do not say, "Richie is putting the blocks in the box and he is sitting in his chair." Instead say, "Richie is putting a block in the box." After assuring yourself that your child accepted having one behavior labeled and watching for a half minute or so, label a second behavior. In general, label only two behaviors during a given "attending" session. When labeling, more is not better.

- Use labels that specify the behavior being observed. This lets the child know that you really are paying attention as opposed to making an offhand comment based on a casual glance . . . "Connie is coloring the rabbit brown," as opposed to saying, "Connie is doing art work." The first labeling describes exactly what Connie is doing. She knows that her mother really is attending. The second label ("You are doing your art work") sounds like Mom has something more important on her mind and is not really attending to what Connie is doing.

- Label only positive behaviors: "You are feeding your dolly," do not say, "You are getting water on the carpet!" To call the child's attention to something like getting water on the carpet is a reprimand. Defiant children get angry when they are reprimanded. As previously mentioned, a reprimand takes money out of your account in your child's bank, weakening the parent–child bond.

- Label sparingly. Do not sound like the running commentary of a sports announcer. If you do talk on and on, your words lose their meaning and significance, and the child stops listening.

When your child consistently accepts having her behavior labeled without showing any adverse reactions, you are ready to move on the second relationship-building skill.

ACCEPTING PRAISE

Most 3-year-old children accept and appreciate being praised for their actions. Indeed, for most children, the best way to get them to do more of an activity or to do the activity better is to praise their work. So Grandmother says to her granddaughter, "Ramona, you are really good at wiping plates. I do appreciate your help!" And Ramona responds by wiping the next plate thoroughly dry. Tell a defiant child that he is doing a good job of wiping the plates dry, and he probably will throw the dish towel and stomp out of the kitchen.

You have probably experienced this very same thing with your child. You praised him, and he had an outburst. Now you know why.

Defiant children dislike praise because they hear praise for what it often is—an attempt to control them. Consider the grandmother who praised Ramona for drying the dishes. Grandmother used praise to keep Ramona at the kitchen sink drying dishes. Since Ramona liked her grandmother, the praise worked. However, if Ramona did not like her grandmother, Ramona would have heard grandmother's praise as an attempt to control her.

Despite the fact that defiant children initially dislike being praised, it is essential that they learn to accept and even value praise. If your child responds adversely when praised, you must teach him this relationship-building skill. Getting your child to accept praise is accomplished by using the same delicate steps recommended for getting your child to accept having his behavior labeled. In other words, the guidelines for praising and for labeling are the same.

The line between praising and patronizing is dangerously thin. Praising is unconditional valuing. Patronizing is praise that is neither deserved nor proportioned. Also, when given correctly, praise is given without an ulterior motive such as getting the child to do a task. Your praise is unconditional. Mrs. Henderson used praise appropriately while her 5-year-old daughter Brenda worked on a puzzle. When Brenda put the last piece into a puzzle, her mother said, "Brenda, you are good at puzzles." In contrast, Mrs. Henderson would have been patronizing and not really praising if she had said, "Brenda, you always do a great job of picking up your room. I know that you will do a good job tonight." As soon as Brenda hears that, she will know that her mother is attempting to manipulate her. Sensing that, Brenda probably won't pick up her room that evening.

A little praise goes a long way. If you praise virtually every positive thing your child does, your words will begin to lose their significance, and your child will stop listening.

Just as your child did not always accept having her behavior labeled, your child will also have times when she reacts adversely to having her behavior praised. When that happens, you must inhibit all signs of disapproval and temporarily discontinue praising. Instead, you revert back to labeling and stay with labeling until your child once again is comfortable. This switching back and forth between praising and labeling will happen several times. So don't be discouraged when you need to retreat a little bit.

In the end, the effort will be worth it. As an additional plus, you will discover levels of patience that you were unaware you possessed!

It is impossible to overemphasize the affect that skillfully given praise will have on your parent–child relationship and how effectively a strong parent–child relationship reduces a child's behavior problems. In our clinical work with defiant children and their parents, we often found that showing the parents how to skillfully give praise and get the child to accept being praised resulted in profound behavior changes. When the children learned to accept praise and the parents learned how to give it, many of the children stopped being noncompliant and defiant.

KEY CONCEPT

Children who feel valued are likely to display socially appropriate positive behavior.

ENGAGING THE CHILD IN COOPERATIVE PLAY

Most 5-year-old children can engage in cooperative play with a friend. If your child is 5 or older, but still cannot participate in cooperative play without getting into squabbles, it is time to teach him this third, relationship-building skill.

When teaching cooperative play, you are no longer a passive observer who occasionally labels behavior or periodically praises it. Instead, you are a participant. Cooperative play goes best when you select an activity that is new to your child. If the activity is not new, your child will think you are butting into his territory. It also helps if this new activity requires more than two hands to complete, or if the activity is labor intensive. For example, assembling a simple model airplane is a good cooperative-play activity because more than two hands are useful for gluing parts together.

When engaging your child in a cooperative activity, the goal isn't doing the task "just right." It isn't even doing the task. Your goal is to have fun together. To keep it fun, do not take a directive role, thereby implying that you know a better way to complete the activity. Your child will not hear your wisdom or appreciate your advice. Instead, he will hear you attempting to control his behavior and to show that you know more than he knows. So if you are using Legos to build a house, and the child starts to build the roof after only three sides have been built, let him. After all, the worst thing that can happen is that the roof will collapse. If such a "disaster" were to happen, quickly strike an upbeat tone. "Wow. That was interesting. Let's build another one." The child will pick up on your energy and enthusiasm and respond accordingly. However, if you said, "That taught us that we need to build four walls before starting on the roof," the child would resent being given advice, and he would stomp off.

When participating with your child in cooperative play, what the child produces, if anything, is irrelevant. What is relevant is your ability to be a nonjudgmental supportive partner. When engaging in cooperative play, never tell your child how to do something, or how not to do something. Remember, you have only one goal when participating in an activity with your child. Your goal is to teach your child that doing things with other people can be fun.

TAKING TURNS

Taking turns is the fourth relationship-building skill. Children who are 6 years old can learn to take turns. So if your child is 6 or older, but still cannot participate in a turn-taking activity, it is time to teach her that relationship-building skill.

Turn-taking is best taught using a task that is the most fun when done with two people. For example, a child can play catch by throwing a ball onto the roof and catching it as the ball rolls off of the edge. But it is more fun to play catch with someone. For 5-year-olds, blowing bubbles is a good turn-taking activity. Dad blows a few bubbles and gestures for his daughter to pop them. Then, watching for cues that his daughter is getting bored with popping bubbles, Dad says, "Let's switch. You blow five bubbles and I will pop them. Then I will blow five bubbles and you can pop them." Good turn-taking activities for older children are shooting hoops with a basketball or putting several golf balls with one putter.

The purpose of taking turns is to teach the child that she can temporarily give up control, but she can soon regain it. For example, in shooting hoops, one person shoots while the other rebounds. The shooter might take three shots, then the roles reverse. It is your turn, and then it is my turn.

Defiant children are initially hesitant to give up control. Suspicion can be read in their eyes. However, if the rule for passing control back and forth is explained in advance, defiant children quickly relax and get into the ebb and flow of having control and then willingly giving it up. When doing turn-taking activities, it is essential that the activity does not morph into a competitive game. For example, taking turns shooting a basketball would become competitive if anyone started tallying who made the most baskets or if someone suggested playing HORSE. A competitive element must be avoided at this stage in the relationship-building process because most defiant children see winning as having power and losing as having no power.

PLAYING A COMPETITIVE GAME

The final relationship skill that defiant children who are 7 years old or older benefit from learning is how to participate in a competitive game and have fun doing it, regardless of the outcome. It is difficult. Even adults playing a friendly game of golf sometimes become so competitive that they throw a golf club, accuse others of cheating, or stomp off the golf course in a fit of anger. If some adults cannot keep a competitive game friendly and enjoyable for everyone involved, imagine how hard it can be for children.

Competitive games are difficult for defiant children because someone always loses. Seeing the similarity between losing a game and losing a power struggle, defiant children want to win every competitive game at all costs.

This relationship skill is best taught using a board game whose outcome depends on chance. In such games, a player's advancement is determined by the spin of an arrow or the roll of dice. Accordingly, half of the time fate favors the parent. But when Dad sees that he is about to win, the worst thing he can do is to cheat in order to lose. The child will see that Dad is cheating. And cheating to lose is still cheating. In the child's mind, if it is okay for Dad to cheat to lose, it surely must be okay for him (the child) to cheat to win. Intentional losing also tells the child that the point of the game is winning. It is not. The point of a competitive game is spending time together so you can enjoy each other's company. Bringing a light-hearted, jovial attitude to the game helps children obtain this perspective.

Modeling.   Teaching a defiant child to play a competitive game is tricky. For starters, the defiant child has a good chance of losing. If he loses, his initial reaction is to get angry. Therefore, the participants should be two mature people and one defiant child. A triad decreases the me-against-you mentality, and it also enables the two adults to work cooperatively to model for the child how to handle the setbacks that are part of the game. For example, in the board game called Trouble, when Mom's marker lands on Dad's square, he can say with an impish smile, "Okay. I go back to the start box. But you better look out because now I will be coming after you!"

Foreshadowing.   During competitive games, something "bad" is likely to happen to the child. Usually, you can see the bad thing that is about to happen before your child sees it. So, if Mom's next roll of the dice could land her on Devin's square, she can say, "Devin, I might land on your square. What are you going to do if that happens?" If Devin is at a loss for a good answer, Dad can help him out. "Well," Dad might say, "Just tell Mom that if she lands on your square and sends you back to the beginning, then she'd better look out for you. You'll be coming up behind her, and it won't be long before you knock her back to the start box." When Mom actually lands on Devin's space, and Devin responds appropriately, it presents the parents with an opportunity to softly praise him. Moreover, if Devin can give a good answer when a parent asks him how he plans to handle a "bad" outcome, he will handle the setback appropriately when it happens.

It is said that art imitates life. Well, a board game also imitates life. In this board game, Mom coached Devin as to how he should respond to an unlucky roll of the dice. When Devin responded in the spirit of the game, his parents conveyed their approval by joking. "Well, Mom," Dad said, "you better look out. Devin is after you!" In the context of the game, Devin will began to look to his parents for hints that "bad" things might be about to happen, and he will also look for subtle guidance about how to respond when a bad thing happens. When your child starts to understand that you have the ability to let him know when bad outcomes are about to happen, and that you can also can give him guidance about how to handle bad outcomes, he will have yet another reason to stop being defiant and to start listening. You can tell when the child is listening to your ability to fore-shadow bad outcomes because he uses this information to display the socially appropriate behavior.

KEYS TO TEACHING RELATIONSHIP-BUILDING SKILLS

When teaching these five relationship-building skills to your child, you must:

- Read and attend to your child's subtle nonverbal signs like muscle tension, jaw tightening, fidgeting, getting red in the face, and other such indicators of tension or agitation.
- Not react to your child's verbal and nonverbal signals of agitation.
- Foreshadow outcomes to help your child respond appropriately.

In our clinic work, we find that many parents initially have a difficult time teaching their child these five relationship-building skills. Their problem is their nonverbal communications. They so badly want their child to accept labeling and to value being praised that when their child does not, the parent's disappointment can be read on their faces. Seeing their parents' disapproval, the defiant child explodes.

So when teaching these relationship skills, you need to work hard at not making any nonverbal reactions that telegraph your disappointment. This is not easy. You may want to ask a friend to observe as you and afterwards give you feedback on your ability to keep a poker face.

CONCLUSION

The first two relationship-building skills are critical. All children must learn to accept having their actions labeled, thereby accepting their parents' attention. Also, every child must learn to accept praise. When your child learns to accept having her actions labeled, and when she comes to appreciate being praised, your relationship will be significantly strengthened. Indeed, we have seen many children in our clinic for whom nothing more is needed. Almost magically, they stop being defiant.

APPLICATIONS

It is difficult to develop and maintain healthy relationships with children who are noncompliant and defiant, but it is imperative.

1. A good place to begin improving the parent–child relationship is by becoming more aware of the nature of your interactions with your child. To do this, make a bracelet for your wrist out of a two-inch slip of paper. Put two headings on the slip, denoting space for counting positive remarks and a space for counting negative remarks. Choose a block of time during the day when you frequently interact with your child. During this time, tally the positive remarks you make and the negative comments you make to your child.

This activity will give a good approximation of the nature of your parent–child interaction, but the data is apt to be biased toward the positive comments because the very act of recording will change your comments. To get a more objective assessment of the parent–child interaction, it would be useful to get a friend or spouse to make the tallies. To add further objectivity, the friend or spouse might make a recording at a time that you are not aware of it. At the end of the time period, examine your recordings. The ratio of positive comments to negative comments should be at least five to one.

Children with strongly embedded defiance often react negatively or even explosively when parents attempt to interact with them, even when the parents make benign comments on the child's behavior. The following activities are designed to help your child accept adult attention, which is the prerequisite for enriched parent–child interactions.

2. Make a list of your child's interests, hobbies, and other things that he does exceptionally well, including any household expectations like going to bed without a fuss or helping put the groceries away.

_____   _____

_____   _____

_____   _____

3. For one week, find five ways to acknowledge the child's accomplishments in these areas without directly praising the child. For example, when the child is within earshot, you might tell your spouse about the accomplishment or tell a grandparent on the other end of the phone. You might display a model she put together or post an art project done at school on the refrigerator door.

4. Does your child sometimes become defiant when you attempt to interact with him or her?

    ___ Yes ___ No

If you checked yes, think about one activity that your child enjoys that creates an opportunity for you to watch, occasionally labeling the child's behavior. Examples of good labeling are, "You are coloring the motorcycle red," or "You are pounding the blocks." In these examples, only one action was identified, and that action was specific. Hearing it, the child knows you are attending.

5. In episodes of roughly two seconds here and four seconds there, watch your child engaging in an activity and label some of his or her behaviors. Immediately complete the following.

    I said,

    "_____."

    My child responded negatively to the labeling by (check behaviors that apply)
        ___ discontinuing the activity.
        ___ briefly pausing.

___ making a facial grimace, showing tension.

___ turning slightly red in the face or neck, or blanching white.

___ showing muscle tension in an arm.

___ glaring at me.

___ actively avoiding eye contact.

___ making a negative comment, like "Go away."

___ breaking or in some way destroying the activity.

My child responded positively to the labeling by (check behaviors that apply)

___ smiling.

___ continuing the activity without interruption.

___ making a positive comment.

___ seeking eye contact.

Your goal is to be able to label two behaviors within a 10-minute period without arousing a negative response from your child.

6. When your child accepts having his or her behavior labeled, you can move on to praising the child. Does your child accept being praised?

___ Yes ___ No

If you checked no, think of an activity your child engages in that will give you opportunities to praise. Examples of praising are: "You are doing a good job of coloring within the lines" or "I like how thoroughly you are brushing your teeth." It is important that the praise is sincere, so wait to praise until your words hit the mark.

While your child is doing a nice job at some activity or task, praise a specific aspect of his or her efforts. Complete the following.

I said,

"_____."

My child responded negatively by (check behaviors that apply)

    ____ discontinuing the activity.

    ____ briefly pausing.

    ____ showing a facial grimace, indicating tension.

    ____ turning slightly red in the face or neck, or blanching white.

    ____ glaring at me.

    ____ turning away to avoid eye contact.

    ____ making a disengaging comment like, "Go away."

    ____ breaking or in some way destroying the activity.

My child responded positively by (check behaviors that apply)

    ____ smiling.

    ____ continuing the activity without interruption.

    ____ seeking eye contact.

    ____ making a comment designed to extend the interaction.

Your goal is to able to praise three behaviors in a one-hour period without arousing a negative response from your child. However, at your child's first indication of a negative response to being praised, disengage. Upon next commenting on your child's behavior, revert back to labeling his or her behavior and stay at that level until the child's behavior indicates acceptance.

It is important not to get discouraged. In may take a while for you to do a good job of labeling and praising, and for your child to accept having his or her behavior labeled or praised.

4

Stop Saying, "Stop That!"

Defiant children seem to constantly do things they shouldn't. When they do, their parents often yell, "Stop that!" But "Stop that!" commands seldom stop anything. In fact, you might have noticed that when defiant children are told to "Stop that," they often increase the rate and the intensity of the unwanted behavior. While there are many ways to say, "Stop that," there is no good way that works with defiant children.

"Stop that!" commands come in many different forms. A parent who says, "Knock it off" is making a "Stop that!" command. A mother who shrieks, "Act your age!" is giving a "Stop that!" command. A dad who growls, "That's enough!" is issuing a "Stop that!" command.

"Ross, Stop That!"

At 3 years of age, Ross could climb, jump, and tumble like an acrobat. When he was 4, Ross could bounce high enough on his bed to do a full flip. He also could climb the kitchen table, leap to the counter, and scale the refrigerator.

When Ross was 5, he climbed up the shelves of his dad's tall bookcase, crouched on top, and jumped onto the couch. Riding the bounce from the couch's springs upward, he did a full flip and landed feet first on the floor. Wow! That was neat. So he did it again and again and again.

Hearing loud thumps at periodic intervals, Mrs. Grimes stopped cooking in order to investigate. Coming into the living room, she saw Ross starting to climb up the bookcase. "Ross," she called out. "Stop that!" He climbed faster. As he perched on top, his mother pleaded, "Ross, dear, come down from there." Instead, Ross jumped from the bookcase, landed on the couch, and did a full flip. With his mother chasing him, Ross scampered down the hall.

Not only are "Stop that" commands ineffective, but every emotion-laden directive tears at the fabric of the parent–child relationship. Since strengthening the parent–child relationship is the secret of decreasing your child's noncompliance and defiance you need to avoid saying "Stop that!"

> **KEY CONCEPT**
>
> "Stop that!" commands weaken the parent–child relationship.

TWO WAYS TO STOP SAYING, "STOP THAT!"
1. PICK YOUR BATTLES

One way to stop saying, "Stop that!" is to pick your battles. Your child probably has a behavior, like throwing her coat on the floor instead of hanging it up on its hook, that aggravates you to no end. But while cluttering the hall is aggravating, it doesn't hurt anyone, nor does it threaten to break anything. It is merely a nuisance behavior. Using punishment to terminate a nuisance behavior is not worth the expenditure of the hard-earned, relationship dollars you have in your account. For example, if Jimmy walks through the living room snapping his fingers, Dad must refrain from saying, "Knock it off! I'm reading the paper." If Rusty teases his teenage sister by imitating how she puts on her lipstick, Mom should not scold him by saying, "Leave your sister alone." These are trivial issues. All children do them. At the moment, the behavior can be ignored.

Furthermore, your child is probably trying to annoy you. So don't let him push your emotional buttons. If you do not respond, you will be amazed when the aggravating behavior simply disappears.[42]

However, most children have one or two aggravating behaviors that either Mom or Dad just can't ignore. If this describes your reaction to one or two of your child's behaviors, you probably feel compelled to respond. But how do you respond without saying those dreaded words, "Stop that"?

One good way to respond to aggravating nuisance behaviors is by modeling the behavior you want to see. For example, a 7-year-old boy stands up and reaches the length of the dinner table to get another helping of mashed potatoes. He should know better, but apparently he doesn't. The child needs to learn table manners. A good way to teach etiquette is by example. So Dad ignored his son's poor manners. He waited a few minutes and said, "Son, would you please pass me the mashed potatoes?" The boy got the message, and he was taught the lesson in a manner that allowed him to retain his dignity. After taking a few bites of mashed potatoes, the boy said, "Hey, please pass me the bread."

Giving a head nod, Dad replied, "Sure thing, Son."

But let's be realistic. While modeling is a good way to teach the child a more appropriate behavior, modeling works slowly. So do not expect that the first time you model the right response, your child will begin to display the desired behavior. It takes time for modeling to have an impact.

2. IGNORE AND REDIRECT

Some behaviors absolutely cannot be overlooked. You can't turn a blind eye on behaviors that

- Could hurt someone.
- Could damage property.
- Stop people from enjoying their basic rights to enjoy their home.

However, even when such serious situations arise, yelling, "Stop that!" seldom stops a defiant child. In these situations you should try a technique known as Ignore and Redirect.

Ignore.   In this context, ignore does NOT mean that you don't see what is happening. Ignore means that while you see what is happening, you do not emotionally react. You keep outwardly cool and collected while you redirect the child.

Ignoring sounds simple, but it is surprisingly difficult to ignore—truly ignore—your child's inappropriate behavior. When your child is doing something wrong or failing to do something right, you probably unwittingly flash a nonverbal reaction that signals your disapproval. You may raise an eyebrow, tighten your jaw, or purse your lips. Defiant children do not miss even the smallest indicator of disapproval. Seeing it, they often escalate the very behavior you want them to stop doing. So if you don't contain your emotions and cannot mask them, your child will see your disapproval. If that happens, the child will escalate his behavior and you won't have a chance to redirect him.

When you ignore, you don't make the slightest reaction—nothing. This takes practice. Think of a specific behavior that your child does that could hurt someone or could damage property. When it happens, what are the nonverbal ways that you signal your disapproval? Do you purse your lips? Do you scowl? Possibly you shrug your shoulders. Whatever your indicators of disapproval are, you need to stop doing them.

KEY CONCEPT

If your child sees that you disapprove of what he or she is doing and are upset, he or she will not accept a redirection.

Redirect.   When your emotions are in check, you are ready to redirect your child's behavior. There are three ways to redirect a child. . .

Redirect Method 1: Give an Alpha Command.   You can issue an Alpha Command. An Alpha Command is a clear concise directive for a specific appropriate behavior.[43] A good Alpha Command requests only one action and that action is observable. Everyone, including the child, knows whether he or she performed the action. A good Alpha Command requests a response that is incompatible with the unacceptable behavior. Finally, when used to redirect a behavior, a good Alpha Command requests an action that the child is likely to do.

For example, imagine that a 10-year-old boy is winding up to throw a baseball from across the room into the living room sofa. Clearly, if he misses the sofa, something is likely to get broken. So, his parent must intervene. But it won't help to call out, "Stop that!" Instead, his dad calmly said, "Get my glove from the box in the garage and I'll play catch outside with you."

This is an Alpha Command because Dad requested one specific action—get my glove—the action requested was observable, and it called for a socially appropriate behavior. It was also a good Alpha Command because if the child goes to get the glove, he will no longer be positioning himself to throw the baseball at the couch. The child can either throw his baseball or he can go get Dad a glove, but he cannot do both.

At this point, you might be shaking your head. The child is doing something terrible, and his Dad is giving him an Alpha Command that directs the child to engage in a fun activity? Yes. Remember your purpose. Your purpose is to get the unacceptable behavior disrupted as quickly as possible. Does the child need to learn not to throw the baseball in house? Absolutely. But this is not the time or place to teach that lesson. The lesson can be taught later in the day when the parent is calm and the child is ready to listen.

KEY CONCEPT

Defiant children will not comply with harshly given, demanding Alpha Commands.

Since there are Alpha Commands, it won't surprise you to learn that there are also Beta Commands. Basically the definition of a Beta command is that it isn't an Alpha Command. There are a number of ways you can fall into the trap of giving Beta commands. Here are some of the common traps.

- Asking a question: "*Would you like to get my glove so we can go out-side and play catch?*"

    When the child is about the throw a ball in living room, you really are not *asking* if he will get your glove. After all, would be okay if he took your comment as a question, and said, "No"?

    Instead of asking a question, the parent should give a directive— "Get my glove . . ."

- Putting together a string of two or more Alpha Commands: "*Hand me the ball, put your truck away, and go brush your teeth.*"

    A string of Alpha Commands needs to be avoided because they do not focus the child's attention on the one action that you need to have happen right now.

- Issuing a vague command where it would be a judgment call as to whether your child actually listened to you: "*Clean up this mess.*"

    Parents know precisely what they mean by "clean up this mess." However, a child does not know. An Alpha Command would be, "Put your plate in the dishwasher."

- Using language figuratively instead of literally: "*Straighten up.*"

    When told to "straighten up," many young children do know the specific response the parent is looking for. An Alpha Command would be "Stand beside me as we wait in line."

It takes practice to become good at giving Alpha Commands. And it also takes practice for children to comply with them. This practice is best done in role plays. For children younger than 8, the practice can be done by playing Simon Says. In the course of the Simon Says game, most of the Alpha Commands are foolish and therefore fun. For example, you might say, "Simon says, 'Do a somersault.'"

Despite the foolishness of the request, there is a serious component. The game establishes the command–compliance connection. It also teaches your child that complying with your requests results in being valued. As your child gets into the game, you can intersperse the fun, humorous Simon-says actions with actions that will, at a later time, be requested. For example, you might say, "Simon says, 'Brush your teeth,'" or "Simon says, 'Sit on the chair,' or "Simon says, 'Put your plate in the sink.'"

The Simon Says game also gives you and your child an opportunity to participate in taking turns, which is one of the relationship-building skills.

In that spirit, your child occasionally gets to be Simon and you have to comply with Simon's request.

For a child older than 8, Simon Says probably won't work. Instead, you need to talk with your child about why certain behaviors are not acceptable in your household and how you will help your child avoid those behaviors. In the Johnson home, this was accomplished by the following conversation:

Preparing Jamal to Accept an Alpha Command

"Jamal," Mrs. Johnson said one quiet evening to her 10-year-old son. "I would like for us to talk about the kinds of things we should not do in our house. Like, what if I was to get mad and throw something across the room? Would that seem right to you?"

"No! You might break something."

"I agree. I shouldn't throw things. I guess no one in this house should get mad and throw things. Do you agree?"

"I guess so," Jamal said sheepishly, knowing that he sometimes got angry and threw things.

"We both know that sometimes you get mad and throw things. I am wondering how I can help. Do you have any ideas?"

"No!" Jamal snapped.

"Well, I can usually tell when you are getting mad. What if I suggested a game when I saw you getting angry? I could say, 'Jamal, get out the checkerboard. Let's play a game.' Do you think you'd get out the checkerboard and we could play checkers for a while, and maybe when the game was over you'd be calmed down?"

"We could see," Jamal replied.

Like all new skills, your child will need to practice complying with a directive. The best way to practice these new skills is by doing role plays. To do a role play, you and your child simply "act out" a situation wherein she is likely to do the specific behavior that is unacceptable to you. While she is pretending to do that behavior, you calmly give the Alpha Command that will redirect her. She complies with the Alpha Command, and you jointly celebrate your collective success at defusing what typically would have been a disaster. You should do at least three such role plays right away and then follow up with several refresher role plays over the next week or two.

Redirect Method 2: Ask a Question.   Another way to redirect a defiant child without having to say, "Stop that!" or even issue a directive, such as happens when giving an Alpha Command, is to ask a question that brings her behavior to her attention. This questioning strategy works because most of the time a defiant child's unacceptable actions are done without really thinking about and without regard to the problems it will cause.

Again, consider the boy getting ready to whip a baseball through his house. It simply does not occur to him that he might miss the couch and the baseball could hit the lamp, breaking it. He probably will not throw the ball if what he is doing is gently called to his attention. The operative word here is *gently*. Gently is accomplished by asking the child a question that causes him to think about what is doing. So Dad asks, "Rusty, where is the best place to practice pitching?"

Rusty will get the point, and he will accept the subtle redirection because the question caused him to evaluate the possible consequences of his action, and it did it in a way that allowed him to retain his dignity. No one told him he was stupid or, for that matter, no one told him what to do. Furthermore, he is apt to accept this type of redirective because it gives him a sense of control.

Of course, when Rusty makes the right decision, Dad quickly acknowledges it. In this case, Dad gave an approving nod as Rusty went to get a baseball glove.

Redirect Method 3: Offer a Choice.   The third way to stop saying, "Stop that!" is to give the child a choice. The choice is always between two equally acceptable alternatives. In the previous example of the boy getting ready to throw a ball in house, Dad could have redirected his son by giving him a choice. "Son," Dad could have said, "would you like to phone your friend Billy and see if he wants to play catch with you or would you like me play catch with you?"

There is something magical about offering a defiant child a choice. The magic is that offering a choice gives him a sense of control. No one is telling him what to do. Instead, the child is choosing what to do. For a defiant child, feeling in control is important.

TWO IMPORTANT CONCEPTS

These redirection techniques are even more powerful and effective when an understanding of early childhood development is woven into your parenting style. Two particularly important principles are allowing for independent decision making and having age-appropriate expectations.

ALLOW CHILDREN TO MAKE THEIR OWN DECISIONS

It is important to allow your child to make many of her own decisions and then learn from that by experiencing that natural consequence of making the decision.[44] When your child makes good decisions, it is easy for you to be supportive and allow your child to make that particular decision. However, it is difficult for you to sit by and say nothing while your child makes poor decisions. Wanting to protect your child from any possible discomfort, you use your "wisdom" to override your child's poor decisions. But protecting your child from making poor decisions is a mistake. Your child will become angry and defiant when you override her decisions. Moreover, when you do not let your child make decisions, you deprive your child of learning to take responsibility for her actions.

> **KEY CONCEPT**
>
> Children learn from making poor decisions.

NATURAL CONSEQUENCES

The best way for your child to learn how to make good decisions is to allow her to experience the natural consequences of making poor decisions. So when your child makes a decision, you want to be sure she experiences what happens as a result of that decision. Most poor decisions lead to natural consequences that are admittedly unpleasant, but they are almost never catastrophic.

Sandra Gets Chilly

It was October 15th. During the dead of the night, the first cold snap of the year sneaked into town. That morning, Sandra headed out the door to play in the backyard. She wasn't wearing a coat. Her Mom grabbed her as she opened the door and said "Hey, it's cold out. Put a coat on!"

"Nah," Sandra in replied. "I won't get cold." But Mom said, "You're not stepping one foot out of this house until you put a coat on!" In order to get out of her mother's grasp and out the door, Sandra complied. Her mother had successfully prevented her daughter from getting chilled. But as measured in relationship dollars, it was an expensive coat that she put on Sandra's back. Of equal concern, Mom prevented Sandra from learning to take responsibility for her own welfare.

If Sandra had gone outside without a coat, the natural consequence would have been getting cold—no big deal. When Sandra felt cold, she would come into the house to get a coat.

Thomas Edison understood the value of learning from natural consequences. One day the great inventor was giving a very important person a tour of his laboratory, showing his visitor projects that were under way as well as successful creations. When they got to the light bulb, Edison said, "That was my most difficult invention. I tried 10,000 times before I got the bulb to give off light without burning up."

"That is an incredible number of mistakes," the visitor mused.

"No!" Edison replied testily. "I did not make 9,999 blunders. I had 9,999 learning experiences that guided me to the right solution."

> **KEY CONCEPT**
>
> Allow children to make decisions and then experience the natural consequences.

Like Edison, parents need to appreciate the teaching value of natural consequences. If Sandra's mother had trusted the teaching ability of natural consequences, Sandra would have learned that when it's cold outside, a coat feels good. As the situation unfolded, the only thing Sandra learned was that her mother was terribly controlling, and she resented her mother for that.

Even some skilled behavior therapists do not understand the teaching value of natural consequences. *Nanny 911* is a popular television show about a professional English nanny who goes to the homes of families whose children are out of control. Nanny analyzes the interpersonal dynamics and then suggests, models, and coaches the parents in how to change the children's "naughty" behavior. The program is a rich source of useful ideas to parents who are raising children with challenging behavior problems. However, even Nanny does not appreciate the teaching power of natural consequences.

A case in point was Nanny's recommendation for a young boy who consistently refused to eat the food that his mother had prepared for supper. Nanny insisted that the boy eat at least one bite of every food item. When the boy didn't, Nanny made the boy sit on the "naughty chair." Why did Nanny do this to the boy? It certainly wasn't out of concern for the child's health. The strapping young boy did not have any unmet nutritional or caloric needs. Instead, Nanny's demand was all about control. The child had a venue for saying, "No, I won't," and Nanny determinedly replied, "Yes, you will. I will make you!" That was an unfortunate power struggle. The boy was refusing to eat merely to push his mother's emotional button. At Nanny's recommendation, the parents used physical force to impose their will on the child, which is a dangerous technique with defiant children. It is dangerous because many defiant children will not back down. I have seen cases where parents used the threat of punitive consequences to force their child to eat this or to eat that, and the child resisted. The children resisted so strongly that it was necessary to hospitalize them for life-threatening weight loss.

In this televised case, there was no need for Nanny to use punitive techniques to coerce the child into eating. The parents could have dealt with the eating problem by creating the conditions so that the child's easiest, most natural response was the right response. All the parents had to do was to make sure that the boy came to the supper table hungry—really hungry. The parents could have done this by removing all junk food from the kitchen, and then making sure that the boy got some exercise when he came home from school. Perhaps he and an older brother could have gone on a long bike ride. Physiology being what it is, the boy almost certainly would have come to the supper table ravenously hungry, and he would have eaten heartily from nearly everything on the table.

But for the sake of making the point, let's extend this example. What if the defiant boy was still a finicky eater that evening? If the parents ignored his finicky eating, the boy would have experienced the natural consequence of his decision. He would have left the table hungry—no big deal. He wasn't going to die. We can be certain that in the morning he would eat what his mother prepared for breakfast.

KEY CONCEPT

Rather than have a power struggle with a child over his or her behavior, engineer the environment so that the response you want from the child is the easiest, most natural one for him or her to make.

Do Not Rescue

Wanting the best for their offspring, many parents rescue their children from experiencing the natural consequences of making poor decisions. Children quickly figure this out, and they take advantage of it. Defiant children masterfully manipulate their parents into making them (the children) do what they should do in the first place, and then they hold it against their parents.

Rescuing Cody

When Cody was 7 years old, he daily resisted his mother's efforts to get him ready for school. When the alarm rang, he shut it off and went back to sleep. To get Cody going, his mother had to pull him kicking and screaming out of bed. Once out of bed, Cody ran to the living room and flicked on the TV. Lying on the floor, he squirmed and fussed while his mother dressed him. When she called him for breakfast, Cody refused to come. She had to drag him away from the television and hold him in his chair so he would eat breakfast. Then she pushed Cody into the bathroom, where she brushed his teeth and combed his hair. When the bus was coming down the lane, she thrust Cody's backpack in his hand and shoved him out the door.

I suggested to Cody's mother that she allow Cody to experience the natural consequence of not getting ready for school. "What would the natural consequence be?" she asked, skeptically.

"Missing school."

"Oh, that would never work!" she mockingly exclaimed. "Cody hates school. Nothin' he'd love better than to stay home with me all day." But after more discussion, she agreed to try it.

Sure enough, the first day Cody missed the school bus and stayed home all day. But the next day, Cody was ready and watching out the window for the school bus. That was six years ago. Since then, Cody has not once missed school because he wasn't ready.

A Qualifying Factor

Allowing children to make decisions and then experience the natural consequences of that decision has exceptions. Children cannot be allowed to make decisions where they could hurt themselves, that could hurt other people, or that could destroy property.

Age-Appropriate Expectations

In our work with defiant children and their parents, we commonly find parents who whose expectations for their child's self-help skills are too high. For example, we find parents who expect 4-year-olds to dish food from a bowl to their plate or pour milk into their cup. Four-year-olds are not capable of that. When the parents expect it, two problems result. First, the parents become frustrated and even angry at the child's failure. Second, the child is upset because he failed to do what his parents expected.

It is necessary to have realistic expectations for your child's self-help skills. For example, 3-year-old children cannot completely dress themselves. They put on socks that do not match. They wear dress shoes with old jeans. They cannot tie their shoes. Four-year-old children cannot dish out food from a bowl or pour beverages from bottle. Five-year-olds cannot dress appropriately for the weather. And so on.

If you are not sure what self-help skills to expect from your child, ask a preschool teacher, an Early Start teacher, a Head Start teacher, or a kindergarten teacher.

CONCLUSION

In order to develop a strong parent-child relationship, it is necessary to avoid reprimanding your child. A commonly used reprimand is saying, "Stop that!" You can use one of two techniques to stop saying, "Stop that!" You can

1. Pick your battles, meaning pay no attention to nuisance behaviors.
2. Ignore the unacceptable behavior while redirecting by
   - Issue an Alpha Command.
   - Ask a question.
   - Offer a choice.

Right now you are probably asking, "Just how does anyone make such calm, cool, collected redirections when a child is about to do something that is likely to hurt someone or break property?" You are exactly correct. None of us are capable of these wonderful responses at the moment of impending disaster. But is this behavior something your child has never done before? No! You already know what things your child does that could hurt someone or could damage property. So think about how you intend to respond the next time you see your child doing that unacceptable behavior. Just as you had your child role play, you role play how you will redirect each of your child's unacceptable behaviors.

APPLICATIONS

There are three ways to stop saying, "Stop that!" The first way is to identify the behaviors the child often displays that are irritating, but can be ignored.

1. Make a list of your child's behaviors that, while aggravating, can be ignored.

_____

_____

_____

_____

2. Are there any behaviors on this list that your child seems to do in order to push your emotional button? _____ Yes _____ No

   If yes,

   What Behaviors?   **How Do You Usually Respond?**

   _____   _____

   _____   _____

   _____   _____

3. When your child exhibits an aggravating behavior, what are your nonverbal signals of disapproval?

   Behavior   **Nonverbal Disapproval**

   _____   _____

   _____   _____

4. What behaviors does your child display that are apt to escalate to the point that someone gets hurt, property gets damaged, or people's basic rights get stomped on?

_____   _____

_____   _____

_____   _____

5. Write out four good Alpha Commands that you are likely to have to issue in order to redirect a behavior so that no one gets hurt, property does not get destroyed, and basic rights are protected.

The Behavior

Example: Child is using a knife to open a box.

The Alpha Command to Redirect the Behavior

"Please hand me the knife."

_____   _____

_____   _____

_____   _____

6. If your child does not tend to comply with verbal directives, consider the same likely behaviors and how you can offer the child two acceptable responses. In other words, give the child a choice.

Example: Child is playing with a knife.

"Please hand me the knife or use the scissors to open the box."

_____   _____

_____   _____

_____   _____

7. Similarly, when your child is displaying an unacceptable behavior, what question could you ask that would prompt him or her to evaluate that behavior and make a better decision?

Example: Child is   "Is there anything else in the
playing with a knife.   drawer that would work better
                           to open the box?"

_____   _____

_____   _____

_____   _____

8. What are some poor decisions that your child is apt to make and what are the natural consequences of those decisions?

Decision	Natural Consequence
• Not dressing appropriately for the weather	Getting cold, wet, or hot
• Not doing homework	Getting a low grade
• Not eating a meal	Getting hungry
• Wearing dirty clothes	Friends may avoid or make remarks

_____   _____

_____   _____

_____   _____

9. Identify the unacceptable decisions that your child tends to make that have the potential to harm other people, damage property, or harm your child and therefore he or she is not allowed to make.

• Not responding to calls to come into the house as bedtime approaches

- Using art supplies, such as permanent markers, on furniture or walls

- Riding a tricycle in the street

- Hitting or kicking other people

- Throwing things in anger

- _____

- _____

5

The Value of Routines

A routine is an unvarying procedure for accomplishing daily tasks/expectations such as picking up toys, taking a bath, and getting into bed. Developing and implementing a routine is the single most effective thing you can do to help your defiant child. Having a schedule allows you to eliminate the one thing that causes a defiant child to have an outburst—telling him or her what to do. Once a schedule is implemented and operating, defiant children come to rely on it. They learn to like their routine because it gives a portion of their day predictability. Behaviorally challenged children like their schedule because it helps them behave. When things are going badly, the routine seems to call out to them. "Hey," it says, "the path to good behavior is over here."

It takes an up-front outlay of time and energy to develop and implement a good routine. However, the startup cost is worth it. A good schedule immediately makes a huge difference in your child's behavior, saving you time and lowering your stress. Most importantly, with a routine in place, you no longer have any more of those destructive battles with your child to get him or her to do necessary tasks.

> **KEY CONCEPT**
>
> Implementing a routine is the singlemost useful thing you can do to help your child.

It is neither necessary nor useful to develop a schedule for the entire day. Instead, develop a routine for those times of the day that your child is particularly likely to have behavior problems. Typically, the difficult times are either in the morning or just before bedtime. If your child is having behavior problems during both of these times, pick one and start there.

HOW TO DEVELOP ROUTINES THAT WORK

USE THE PREMACK PRINCIPLE

In 1959 David Premack, a psychologist, discovered that rats would press a bar that stuck out into their cage if pressing the bar gave them the opportunity to run in a revolving wheel.[45] The discovery that rats would perform an uninteresting activity (bar pressing) in order to earn the opportunity to do a high-interest activity (running in a revolving wheel) came to be called the Premack Principle. The formulation of the Premack Principle caused some people to wonder whether their grandmother was a psychologist. After all, she used a similar approach with them. "You have to eat your green beans," many children were told by their grandmothers, "before you get ice cream."

Whether it is called the Premack Principle or Grandmother's Rule, the concept is the same. In a well-planned routine, the child has to complete several, low-interest activities in order to get to do a high-interest activity. Put another way, a schedule requires children to get their work done before they play.

When the Premack Principle was applied to Brent's evening activities, a portion of the routine read:

8:00	Bath
8:25	Put on pajamas
8:30	Bedtime snack

In this section of the routine, Brent had to take a bath, something he often balked at doing, and he had to put on his pajamas before he got his bedtime snack.

Prior to implementing this schedule, the evening was a disaster. When his mother told Brent to take a bath, he typically had a temper tantrum. Faced with Brent's tantrum, Mom usually withdrew the request. "It's no big deal," she tried to assure herself, "if he misses a bath now and then." However, at other times Mom insisted that Brent take his bath, and her demand precipitated a battle.

A routine changed that lose–lose, parent–child power struggle. With the schedule in place, Brent realized that if he wanted his bedtime snack, he had to take a bath. Hence, the routine took Mom out of the enforcement role, and it made Brent responsible for taking a bath in order to earn his snack. With the routine in place, failure to get his bedtime snack was a natural consequence that fell on Brent if he chose to be noncompliant.

> ### KEY CONCEPT
>
> By using a routine, you do not have to force and coerce your defiant child to do necessary tasks.

ESTABLISH THE RIGHT PAYOFF

Meaningful.   The payoff must be meaningful to the child. But meaningful does not mean essential. Brent might like a bedtime snack, but he can live without it. Yet his desire for a bedtime snack motivates him to complete two, low-interest activities to earn it.

Under Parent's Control.   The payoff must be under the parent's control. If your child is likely to go into the kitchen and fix his own bedtime snack, a snack will not work as a payoff. A bedtime snack will only work as a payoff if your child depends on you to prepare it and put it on the table.

Putting a Payoff under a Parent's Control

Paul insisted on watching a particular television program every morning as he got ready for school, and this caused problems. When the TV program came on, Paul stopped getting ready for school and plunked himself in front of the television. When Mom tried to get Paul back on track, he had a temper tantrum.

The television was a powerful incentive, but it was not under Mom's control. So she made two changes:

1. Every morning the television set in the living room was made inoperable by flipping the fuse that powered the outlets in the living room.

2. The small television set on the kitchen counter was moved to the top of the refrigerator.

Eureka! Mom now had control over the delivery of a powerful payoff. In order to watch his television show, Paul had to show up in the kitchen dressed and ready for school.

KEY CONCEPT

All payoffs have to be under your control.

USE ROUTINES TO SOLVE CHRONIC BEHAVIOR PROBLEMS

It is important to use routines creatively to solve chronic behavior problems. Bedtime is a case in point. Parents of behaviorally challenged children often struggle every night to get their children to bed and then have them stay in bed. Prior to implementing an evening schedule, this is how bedtime went at the Coleman house.

Casey's Bedtime

It was 9:00 when Mrs. Coleman said to her 9-year-old son, Casey, "It's time to head to bed."

"No!" Casey yelled back. Ignoring his mother's directive, he plopped himself in front of the television in the living room. An hour later, his dad, said, "Casey, it is far past your bedtime. Now get to bed, and I mean business." In response, Casey went to his room and he shut the bedroom door. But instead of going to bed, he got out his toys. Seeing the light creep under the door to Casey's bedroom, his Dad came in. Grabbing Casey by the arm, he put his son to bed and gave him a good swat on the behind. "Now stay there!" Dad said.

Casey's bedtime problem could be solved with a routine. In this case, the routine would read:

8:45	Brush teeth
9:00	Bedtime
9:05	Story time
9:20	Lights out

If Casey was in bed at 9:05, a parent would lie by him and read to him for fifteen minutes. As with all payoffs, there is a window of opportunity. So reading time would not start until Casey was in bed and that window of opportunity closed at 9:20, when it was time for lights out.

MAKE MAXIMUM USE OF THE PREMACK PRINCIPLE

You must make maximum use of all the available payoffs. For example, prior to thinking about a routine for Jason, his parents did not make use of Jason's interest (insistence would be a better word) in watching his favorite program on Nickelodeon as a tool to get him to help with pickup. Therefore, every evening Jason watched his favorite TV program. After it was over, his parents tried to get him to pick up the toys in his room. Of course, he wouldn't.

When they implemented a routine, things changed. Now, watching the TV show depended on Jason picking up his toys during family pickup time. This demonstrates two important points about routines:

- High-interest activities should not be given away. They should be used as incentives for children to do low-interest tasks.
- If a child has little interest in doing a particular task, it must be immediately followed by a payoff he really wants.

INVOLVE THE CHILD

If possible, involve your child in the development of the routine. After Mrs. Sanders thought about a plausible routine for her 8-year-old daughter, she said, "Cassandra, when you have your bedtime snack this evening, I'd like to get your ideas on something. Can you remind me of that?" It was no accident that Mom scheduled the discussion for snack time. She and Cassandra were much more likely to have a discussion if she had a reason to stay at the table.

Involving Cassandra

"Cassandra," Mrs. Sanders said as they sat at the table, "I would like us to write out what happens every evening from after supper until you go to bed. Right after supper there is the family pickup time. What do you do after that?"

"I watch my show on Nickelodeon," Cassandra said defiantly, as if expecting a directive or ultimatum.

"Right," Mom replied, conspicuously writing that down. "When your TV show is over at 8:00, what comes next?

"You make me take a bath," Cassandra snapped.

Ignoring the tone of Cassandra's answer, Mom cheerfully said, "Right. And by 8:25 you are getting into your pajamas. What comes next?"

"My bedtime snack."

"And after your bedtime snack?"

"Brush my teeth," Cassandra reported.

"Brush teeth," Mom repeated, writing it down on the paper. "Then it is time for bed, and we try to get to bed by 9:00. But there is one thing that I'd like to add."

"What's that?" Cassandra asked defensively.

"I would like to add a reading time—a time when I read a story to you. Would you like that?"

"Can I pick the book?"

"Certainly."

Cassandra's resultant routine was:

6:30	Family pickup
7:00	TV
8:00	Bath
8:25	Pajamas
8:30	Bedtime snack
8:50	Brush teeth
9:00	Bed
9:05	Story time
9:20	Lights out

Establish a Clear Finish

All activities in a routine must have a clear finish. A clear finish means that it is obvious to everyone when the activity is completed. For example, the bedtime snack has a clear finish. The snack is over when the food is eaten. But some activities do not have a clear finish. For example, what is a clear finish to bathing? The bath isn't over when the bath water is gone. Since bath time does not have a clear and obvious finish, you have to establish one. If you don't, you will be forced to tell your child to get out of the bathtub. But telling him to get out of the bathtub probably will result in a tussle, further damaging the parent–child relationship.

Cassandra's reading time was a situation where a clear finished was needed.

Cassandra's Temper Tantrum

Mom had read to Cassandra for about ten minutes when she reached the end of chapter two. Seeing the end of the chapter as a good place to stop reading, Mom announced "That's it for tonight," and she started to leave the bedroom. But before Mom got out the bedroom door, Cassandra whimpered, "Read more . . . please."

"No!" Mom replied firmly. "That was the end of the chapter. I am not reading any more tonight." And she left, closing the door behind her. But Cassandra did not accept no for an answer. When her mother walked out of the bedroom, Cassandra got out of bed and followed Mom into the living room.

"Read just a little more, and I will go to bed. I promise," she pleaded.

"No!" Mom firmly replied. At that, Cassandra threw herself on the floor, pounding her fists and screaming. The baby woke, crying. Mom knew that if she did not read a little more, Cassandra would continue screaming and the baby would keep crying. So Mom gave in. Of course, giving in to her daughter's demand further reinforced Cassandra for having temper tantrums.

Visual Indicators. Mom could have used a visual indicator to create a clear finish to reading. A red card is a good visual indicator to signal a finish. Early the next evening, Mom should have this conversation with Cassandra:

Establishing a Clear Finish

"Cassandra," Mom would say as they were having their bedtime snack, "tonight we will read to the end of chapter three. I have a big piece of red paper that will tell us when we are at the end of chapter three. Here," Mom might say, opening the book to the end of chapter three, "could you place this piece of red paper at the end of chapter three?" When Cassandra did so, Mom would comment, "Good. When we reach the end of chapter three, the piece of red paper that you placed there will remind us that reading time is over. I will give you a big hug, and leave. On the way out, I will turn off the lights so that you can go to sleep."

KEY CONCEPT

All activities in the routine should either have a clear finish or be given a clear finish.

Auditory Indicators.   A tone or a bell is also a way to establish a clear finish for some activities. A kitchen timer works well because it can be set for a specific amount of time, and it rings when the allotted time has passed.

A kitchen timer helped bring Brent's bath time to an end without the typical outburst. Like many children, Brent hated to get into the bathtub. But once he was in the tub, he hated to get out of the tub. Brent would play in bathtub for an hour if his mother would allow it. Therefore, Mom used a kitchen timer to establish a clear finish for bath time. When the timer went off, it was time to get out of the tub. In order to involve Brent in the process of developing a clear finish for bath time and thereby increasing his commitment, Mom had Brent set the timer for fifteen minutes.

Foreshadow the Finish.   Foreshadowing the rapidly approaching end of an activity is like seeing a curve sign when you are driving down a black highway on a moonless night. Both foreshadowing and curve signs help everyone prepare for a sudden change, thereby avoiding disasters. So just before Cassandra's mother reached the end of chapter three, she foreshadowed the upcoming end of reading time. "Cassandra," she said, "we have two pages to read before we reach the end of chapter three and the red piece of paper. What does it mean when we reach the red piece of paper?"

"It means that reading time is over." Cassandra grumbled.

"You are exactly right," Mrs. Coleman replied. "Reading time will be over." After two more pages, Mom reached the red piece of paper. Reaching it, she could have announced, "We are at the red paper. Reading time is over." However, that comment is a statement, and a statement that sounds a lot like a directive. Being sensitive to the importance of not giving verbal directives, Mom did not make that pronouncement. Instead, she said. "We have reached the red paper. What does that mean, Cassandra?"

"The End!" Cassandra exclaimed.

"You're right!"

COMMUNICATING THE ROUTINE

WHY A COMMUNICATION BOARD IS NECESSARY

When defiant children are told what to do, it is as if they hear an invitation to a brawl. "You gonna make me?" defiant children challenge. "Let's see ya." If the parent insists on compliance, the fight is on. And when the parent tries to make the child comply, the child goes to almost any length to win. In the face of the child's resistance, the parent withdraws the directive, and the child wins, making him even more determined not to comply the next time a parent tells him what to do.

The only way the parent can "win" a power struggle is to punish the child so severely that she will knuckle under and comply. However, this "win" comes at the expense of the parent–child relationship. No one, especially a defiant child, likes to be punished. Furthermore, when the parents use their size and strength to punish their child, the child learns a lesson. But it is not a good lesson. The child learns that if you are big enough you can inflict your will on people who are littler than you.

A Communication Board

A communication board allows you to convey your expectations to your child without having to tell her what to do.[46] Your child knows that if you tell her what to do, she can have a temper tantrum and get you to withdraw your directive. But a communication board pays no attention whatsoever to her antics, protests, and temper tantrums.

Two types of communication boards are useful for defiant children: object communication boards and written communication boards.

Object Communication Boards. An object communication board is appropriate for children 6 years old and younger. As the name implies, an object communication board uses an object to communicate an activity. For example, a spoon is a good object to signify that it is time for a bedtime snack. A toothbrush is a good object to signify that it is time to brush teeth. A washcloth is a good object to indicate that is time for a bath. A toy truck can indicate pickup time, and a book can communicate that it is time to head to the bedroom for reading time.

The objects are put on the communication board, which is usually a shelf or a counter at the child's eye level, and they are arranged from left to right—the way we read. (Everything in this system is done from left to right so that it sets up a pattern of how things are done. Once children learn that left to right pattern for doing things, they tend to follow it). Seeing the first object on her left, the child grabs the toothbrush in her hand. The toothbrush tells her where to go (the bathroom), and it also tells her what she will do when she gets there (brush her teeth). The toothbrush in her hand also helps to keep her from getting distracted by interesting things that want her attention as she walks to the bathroom. She might see her cat that needs to be petted. She might hear a television that needs to be watched. Or, she might walk by a doll that needs to be fed. Each of these distracting things has the capacity to draw the child away from the task at hand, setting up a situation where a parent feels compelled to give one of those dreaded verbal directives. However, the toothbrush in the girl's hand continuously creates a compelling combination of tactile, kinesthetic, and visual stimuli that constantly remind her that she needs to brush her teeth.

Furthermore, the toothbrush in her hand creates a compulsion to get the task over with. "This toothbrush must go some place," the child seems to tell herself, "and I must get rid of it." It is as if the toothbrush says, "Take me to the bathroom." Indeed, some 4-year-old children carrying their toothbrushes to the bathroom have been heard whispering to themselves, "brush teeth, brush teeth."

Once in the bathroom, all of the things that the child needs to brush her teeth are laid out. Starting on the left and working to the right, the girl sees toothpaste. Toothpaste belongs on a toothbrush. When toothpaste is on the toothbrush, it only makes sense to the child to brush her teeth. When she is finished, her toothbrush holder is to the right of the sink. To the immediate right of the toothbrush holder is a Check Routine Card, whose function will be explained shortly.

Written Communication Boards.   As soon as children can read, they are ready for a written communication board. Whereas object communication boards are arranged from left to right, written communication boards are too long to string out horizontally. Therefore, written communication boards are arranged from top to bottom. Since children who are beginning to read are also beginning to tell time, a written communication board pairs each activity with a specific time. The words can be written on a poster board that is attached with a hook-and-loop fastener to the communication board.

8:30	Eat snack
8:50	Brush teeth
9:00	In bed
9:05	Read story

By the time children are old enough to read, most of them do not need to carry an object in their hand to get to the place where the task is done. If the word is attached to the poster board by a hook-and-loop fastener, it can be pulled off the communication board and dropped into a shoebox sitting to the right of the communication board. Children who are 8 years old and older can use an even more simplified communication board. Their communication board can be merely a sheet of paper hung in a convenient spot, like the front of the refrigerator, listing the times and activities. When using such a listing of tasks, the child reads the next task that needs to be done, crosses it off the list, and then does the task.

Check Routine Cards

When an activity is over, your child needs to go back to the communication board to learn her next activity. However, getting from her current location back to the communication board is another perilous time. For example, if your child stops to play with a toy, you will be tempted to say, "Go check your routine." There, it happened yet again—you told your defiant child what to do.

The solution is a "Check Routine Card." A Check Routine Card is a big green checkmark put on a 2″ x 2″ piece of poster board. When children finish each activity, they should find a Check Routine Card to their immediate right. So when Sally finishes brushing her teeth and puts her toothbrush into the toothbrush holder, to the immediate right of the toothbrush holder is a Check Routine Card. She takes the card and, as the name implies, goes to the communication board. The Check Routine Card is "matched" to a Check Routine Card taped on a manila envelope posted to the immediate left of the communication board. Seeing the match, Sally deposits the Check Routine Card that she is carrying into the manila envelope.

Again (and always) Involve the Child

Just as it was important to involve your child in developing the routine, it is important that you involve your child in creating the communication board. Start with the first task on the routine. In our sample routine, the first task was helping with family pickup. If your child is 6 years old or younger and using an object communication board, ask, "What would remind you that it is family pickup time? If he does not know, say, "Would a toy car remind you that is family pickup time?"

The next step is to find a place to put the communication board. Object communication boards can be on a shelf or desk top in the child's room. Written communication boards can be put on the front of the refrigerator in the kitchen or the closet door in the child's bedroom. When all is complete, walk your child through several pretend runs (role plays) of the total routine. While doing this, be excited, positive, and supportive.

MAKE THE TASKS DEVELOPMENTALLY APPROPRIATE

It is essential that all of the activities listed on the routine are developmentally appropriate. When defiant children are given a task that is beyond their grasp or ability, they become noncompliant, defiant, and even aggressive. For example, asking a 4-year-old girl at suppertime to pour milk for the family would not be developmentally appropriate. She will spill it. When she does, her mother is apt to reprimand her, causing an outburst. However, putting silverware by each plate is an age-appropriate task for a 4-year-old.

It is hard to predict which low-interest tasks the child won't be able to complete. So start with low-interest tasks that are well within your child's capability. When the routine is well established and operating smoothly, you can slowly introduce more difficult age-appropriate tasks and make adjustments as necessary.

DO NOT DISCONTINUE THE ROUTINE

Typically, the routine goes well. In fact, the routine often goes so well that parents soon begin to think that the child no longer needs it. And they start to take short cuts. For example, they "save time" by not setting out the Check Routine cards. Or they become lenient, allowing the child to get the payoff without adequately completing a low-interest task.

Do not discontinue any element of a successful routine or take shortcuts! If you do, it will be only a matter of time before the child again becomes noncompliant and defiant. In response to the child's noncompliance and defiance, parents often revert to making sharply worded demands and issuing ultimatums. Once started, the downward spiral continues. Soon, you are back to where you started.

BE A HELPER

The parent–child relationship is strengthened every time you help your child be successful. And that is yet another great thing about a routine. The routine provides you numerous opportunities to help your child successfully complete low-interest tasks. This does not mean that you do the low-interest task for the child. Rather, it means that you sometimes assist the child in completing some low-interest tasks, especially tasks like pickup, homework, and possibly bathing, that go better with a little help. The routine also gives you numerous opportunities to affirm your child for completing task. Every time you do, you are putting relationship dollars in your account at the child's bank and are strengthening your relationship with your child.

Assist with Some Tasks Every Day

Assist your child each evening with at least one low-interest activity. By assisting, your actions speak volumes. You are saying, "I am here to help you be successful." While helping your child, find appropriate opportunities to praise and value him. For example, at the end of the task, let's say it was pickup, you say, "You did a great job putting your toys in the toy box. That deserves a big hug!"

> **KEY CONCEPT**
>
> The parent–child relationship is strengthened every time the parent provides meaningful help that contributes to the child's success, and it is also strengthened every time you affirm your child for completing tasks.

Also, help your child with any low-interest tasks that might be challenging for her to complete. For most children, pickup is such a task. Initially, most children cannot fully comprehend the concept of an uncluttered room. So the child probably will not satisfactorily put away her things during the family's evening pickup. So as long as your child is making an effort and is engaged, help. Your efforts and supportive posture will not go unnoticed. When you help your child, she will begin to respond in kind.

Assist the Child with Getting from the End of One Task to the Beginning of the Next. The time between the end of one activity and the beginning of the next activity is particularly difficult for many defiant children, especially those who, by temperament, are impulsive and have short attention spans. So be vigilant at these times, watching for indications that your child needs help getting on with her routine.

Helping Shirley

One evening after her favorite television program was finished, Shirley started leafing through a picture book about dinosaurs, quickly becoming absorbed in the book. Mom could have allowed Shirley to get behind on her routine. But supportive parents do not wait to catch their children being irresponsible and then take satisfaction in the child's failure. Instead of waiting for Shirley to fail, Mom monitored the time. When the clock reached 8:10 and Shirley still had not started her bath, Mom went to the communication board, got a Check Schedule Card from the manila envelope, and, without comment, handed the Check Schedule Card to her daughter. As Shirley took the Check Schedule Card, Mom asked, "Do you want me to start your bath water?"

BE SUPPORTIVE

Your child will occasionally struggle to complete a low-interest task. At those times, you will want to provide that little extra help your child needs to complete a troublesome, low-interest task. For example, one evening Rusty's homework assignment was to find four magazine articles about wild animals. Rusty was having trouble getting motivated to start the assignment. Dad could have put all of the responsibility on his son, and let him fail. But he didn't. Instead, Dad asked, "Rusty, would you like me to find you some magazines that might have articles about wild animals?"

"Ya!"

Dad found some relevant magazines. Handing them to his son, Dad asked, "Do you think these might have some pictures that you need?"

ROUTINES AS LIFE PRESERVERS

A routine gives your defiant child the structure she needs to be successful. When your child comes to realize that, she will increasingly rely on the routine to make it through tough days. When your child momentarily "loses it," the routine is there to tell her what she needs to do to get back on track. Watching an out-of-control child use her routine to compose and organize herself is almost magical. "Hey," she seems to tell herself, "I know how to get out of this mess. I get out by following my routine."

CONCLUSION

Parenting is about empowering children and helping them to become increasingly independent. Routines are one step to independence. Nearly every adult follows a routine to make effective use of his or her time. The only difference is that our daily, around-the-house routine is etched in our mind. It is not written out where everyone can see it. But to help your children establish and follow their routines, it will help if they can see you following your routine. So consider writing out your routine and making it clear to your children that at key times of day you follow it.

APPLICATIONS

Developing and implementing routines is the most useful thing you can do
to help your defiant child. This exercise will help you develop a routine with
your child for a one- or two-hour block of time during the day that is the
most challenging for you and your child.

1. Identify the time of the day when your child is most noncompliant and defiant.

   _____ early morning

   _____ mid morning

   _____ noon

   _____ afternoon

   _____ early evening

   _____ late evening

2. Identify the one or two things that your child needs to do during this time block, but consistently resists doing.

   _____

   _____

3. Identify the payoffs that typically are provided or at least could
   be provided during this time period.

   _____

   _____

4. Is the delivery of each identified payoff currently under your
   control? _____ Yes _____ No

   If no, what can you do to get the payoff under your control?

   _____

   _____

If you cannot do anything to get the payoff under your control, you need to find another payoff.

5. Discuss with your child the activities that typically occur during this time block. With your child's participation, develop a routine that identifies the low-interest activities whose completion leads to the opportunity to do the high-interest activity, i. e., the payoff.

Time   **Activity**

_____   _____

_____   _____

_____   _____

_____   _____

_____   _____

6. Does each activity on the routine have a clear finish?
_____ Yes _____ No
If not, what can you do to give that activity a clear finish?

Activity   **Clear Finish**

_____   _____

_____   _____

_____   _____

7. Select a communication system that is developmentally appropriate for your child.

_____   Object communication system

_____   Written communication system

8. With participation from your child, make a communication board.

9. What activities might your child have difficulty completing?

_____

_____

_____

10. When your child has difficulty completing an activity, what will you do to help the child be successful?

Activity   **Type of Help to Be Given**

_____   _____

_____   _____

_____   _____

11. Complete the following table for one week showing the help you gave your child so that he or she could successfully follow the routine.

	Sun.	Mon.	Tues.	Wed.	Thurs.	Fri.	Sat.
No help							
Routinely helped on							
Helped as needed on							

For the first week and sometimes up to a month, the routine works wonderfully. It is essential to use this honeymoon period of the routine to strengthen your relationship with your child. This is done by praising him or her when he or she checks the communication board, acknowledging the completion of low-interest tasks, and affirming success when payoffs are earned.

12. Using the routine to strengthen the relationship: Complete the following chart for the first week that the routine is implemented. Guard against becoming so mechanical and scripted in your valuing comments and gestures that they become meaningless.

**My Child Did These
Tasks in the Routine   I Valued My Child by**

Monday

_____   _____

_____   _____

_____   _____

_____   _____

Tuesday

_____   _____

_____   _____

_____   _____

_____   _____

etc.

Part II

MANAGING NONCOMPLIANCE AND DEFIANCE

When you implement the prevention measures described in Part I, your child's episodes of noncompliance, defiance, and aggression sometimes simply disappear. And they never return. The resultant harmony can be heard throughout the house, providing parents numerous opportunities to keep the child's conduct problems from reappearing by liberally administering daily doses of praise and valuing.

But more typically, the prevention measures and the novelty of the routine give your child up to a month of really good behavior. Then one day . . . bam. The noncompliant defiant child of a month ago suddenly and unexpectedly returns. What happened, and it almost always happens, is that the previous pattern of behavior reasserts itself. It happens because your child wants to regain control. The reappearance of this behavior will shake your confidence. You will wonder whether the prevention techniques had only a short-term effect and now, just like everything else you have tried, they no longer work. Frustrated and discouraged, you might be tempted to abandon your newly adopted prevention measures. Don't. You are making progress, and you and your child are moving in the right direction. You have just reached the next step in this process.

In Part II, you will learn how to guide your child through any such relapse.

6

Breaking
the Coercive Cycle

Gerald Patterson, one of the early researchers/clinicians in behavior-training programs for parents, believed that when children are markedly defiant, a particular parent–child dynamic is operating. He called this destructive parent–child dynamic the Coercive Cycle.[47]

The Coercive Cycle begins when a parent gives the child a directive. Instead of complying, the child screams, "No!" The child's outburst causes the parent to become angry. With a more stern voice, the parent repeats the directive. But in response, the child becomes even more defiant. He might kick the wall, throw something, holler obscenities, or make threats. Finding the child's behavior unpleasant and upsetting, the parent withdraws the request. When the parent withdraws the request, the child ceases the outburst, which is a huge relief to the parent. The child also feels good. He did not have to comply with the parent's directive.

> **KEY CONCEPT**
>
> When children are chronically defiant, the Coercive Cycle is usually operating.

In a family, the Coercive Cycle might go like this:

Jimmy Gets His Way

"Son, it's time for bed." Jimmy's dad called out, glancing up from the evening paper. "Stop watching TV and get into your pajamas." Jimmy ignored the directive. After a time, Dad repeated the directive, but more sternly. "Hey, it's time for bed! Now get on the move!"

"No. I want to watch the end of *The Terminator!*" Jimmy shouted back from the living room.

"I said now, and I mean it," Mr. Perron said sternly, putting down the newspaper and heading for the living room. Hearing his dad coming, Jimmy ran into the kitchen, where there was another television. Mr. Perron knew that if he pursued Jimmy, it would mean a fight to get him to bed. It had been a tough day at work. Mr. Perron wanted to relax, if only for a few minutes. "You deal with this," he called out to his wife.

"Sure," his wife replied from the laundry room. "As soon as I finish the wash." But the words were offered only to soothe her husband. Glancing at her watch, Mrs. Perron realized that *The Terminator* would be over by the time the wash was done. Then Jimmy would go to bed without a fuss.

This "little" scenario seems harmless. After all, what is the big deal? So Jimmy missed his bedtime by a half hour. That isn't all that important. Or is it? The issue is not that Jimmy got to extend his bedtime by a half hour. The issue is how it happened. Jimmy got to extend his bedtime by intentionally defying a directive. Furthermore, the parents withdrew the request (backed off) because they knew that if they insisted on compliance, Jimmy would have a huge temper tantrum. He would make their evening miserable. The dynamic that unfolded in the Perron household spells trouble. Jimmy made it clear that in "his" house, he does what he wants, when he wants. He is in control, and he will go to any length to keep control.

THE GENESIS OF THE COERCIVE CYCLE

No parent ever sees the seeds of the Coercive Cycle being planted. It happens during a seemingly benign incident that the parents don't even remember. Perhaps the child was loudly pounding wooden pegs with his wooden hammer. Wanting some quiet, Mrs. Hamilton said, "Bryce, that's enough pounding. Find something else to do!" Bryce paused for a minute, waited for his mother to become otherwise occupied, and went back to pounding his pegs. When his mother didn't say anything, Bryce realized that he had gotten away with disobeying his mother. The seed of the Coercive Cycle was planted.

KEY CONCEPT

A Coercive Cycle begins when a parent makes a request of the child, the child refuses to comply, and the parent withdraws the request.

A few days later, Mrs. Hamilton again requested Bryce to stop hammering his pegs. Remembering what worked for him the last time, Bryce stopped hammering for a minute and waited for his mother to shift her attention elsewhere. When she did, Bryce went back to hammering the pegs. But this time Bryce got a surprise. When he started hammering, Mom rushed into the room, angrily yanked the hammer out of his hand, and threw it in the toy box.

That made Bryce furious. As soon as his mother left the room, he got the hammer out of the toy box and started pounding. Mrs. Hamilton heard the loud hammering, but just then the telephone rang. So Mrs. Hamilton let Bryce continue to pound with his hammer while she answered the phone. The Coercive Cycle took root.

Over the next month, this dynamic was frequently repeated. While it was never again about hammering wooden pegs into round holes, Mrs. Hamilton occasionally requested Bryce to do this or that. Increasingly, he did not comply. Each time that Mrs. Hamilton ignored Bryce's noncompliance, the Coercive Cycle gathered strength. One day Bryce and his cousin were in Bryce's bedroom, noisily playing. "Boys," Mrs. Hamilton called out from the living room, "please go outside and play."

"No! We're havin' fun," Bryce yelled back. Immediately, Mrs. Hamilton was out of her chair and headed for Bryce's bedroom, intent on teaching him to obey her directives. But she caught herself. "Best not create a scene in front of my visiting sister-in-law," she thought to herself. So Mrs. Hamilton merely closed the door to Bryce's room, and she went back to the living room. At that moment the Coercive Cycle became entrenched.

KEY CONCEPT

By the time parents recognize that the child has become defiant, the Coercive Cycle is well established.

In its full-blown form, the Coercive Cycle is a power struggle. The parent says, "You will, or else!" The child emphatically replies, "I will not!" Defiant children almost always win the power struggle. They win the power struggle because once a battle begins, defiant children will pay almost any price in order to win. Parents, on the other hand, typically withdraw from the power struggle when the cost of winning becomes higher than they are willing to pay.

The Price of Peace

When the Coercive Cycle was explained at a parent-training session, Mrs. Wong stated that she understood the Coercive Cycle very well. "I live it," she said. "Just last night it was 9:30, well past Clifford's bedtime. From the kitchen, I heard him put a disk into the DVD player. 'Turn off that DVD right now and get to bed!' I called out in my sternest tone.

"Ten minutes later, I went into the living room. Clifford was watching a movie. Picking up a magazine, I gave him a good swat on his bottom. 'I told you to turn off that DVD and get to bed, and I meant it.'

"Yelling like I had beaten him with a stick, Clifford rolled over and raked his fingernails down my leg, drawing blood. I swatted him hard along side the head with the newspaper. He screamed louder and even tried to bite me.

"I walked away. I realized that I was giving in to him, and I knew that giving in to him was wrong, but it had been a long hard day. I desperately needed a few moments of peace."

Mrs. Wong got her few moments of peace. Initially, those moments of peace were bought at a cheap price. But now, the price of peace is expensive. Tomorrow the cost will be exorbitant. Even when the dynamic is pointed out to parents and they see how devastating it is to their family, many parents find it difficult to break the Coercive Cycle. **But the coercive cycle must be broken.**

THE CONVENTIONAL WISDOM FOR BREAKING THE COERCIVE CYCLE

One approach for breaking the Coercive Cycle might be called a frontal assault. A frontal assault is an unblinking unrelenting attack right into the teeth of the child's defiance. A frontal assault pits you against your child in a test of wills. It is a power struggle.

> ### KEY CONCEPT
>
> A frontal assault on the Coercive Cycle is a parent–child power struggle.

Some behavior specialists advocate using a frontal assault to break the Coercive Cycle.[48,49] A frontal assault is, at least in theory, simple and straightforward. It's all about rewards and punishment. Parents are told that when they give their child a directive, he or she must do it. Even if the child has a temper tantrum, they cannot withdraw the directive. Parents cannot withdraw the directive because that would reward the child for having a temper tantrum. So parents are told that instead of withdrawing the directive, they must punish the child until he or she complies.

The tools of a frontal assault are seductively simple. All parents have to do is acquire the resolve to never retreat after they make a directive. If the child refuses to comply, they punish him or her until he or she obeys.

When the dynamics of the Coercive Cycle are pointed out to parents, they are embarrassed to discover that their child is running the household. An inner voice chastises them, saying, "For Pete's sake! Are you going to let a mere kid get the best of you? You're the parent, aren't you?" Spurred by this self-imposed guilt, many parents are drawn into the inevitable power struggle like a moth is drawn into a flame.

THE DANGERS OF MAKING A FRONTAL ASSAULT ON THE COERCIVE CYCLE

When parents make a frontal assault, they join their child in a power struggle. Someone wins and someone loses. The winner is the person who can punish the most. Often, this is the child. If the child throws a big enough temper tantrum, causes enough commotion, or creates enough embarrassment, the parents usually withdraw the request. When the parents do, they lose. And when the parents lose, the child wins. Rather than putting an end to the Coercive Cycle, parents end up strengthing it.

Parents often lose when they make a frontal assault for two reasons. The first reason is that they are not prepared for the level of violence that a defiant child will resort to in order to win the power struggle. For example, one parent who came to us for assistance related what happened when she tried to make her child comply with the simple directive to "go to bed." When she told her child to go bed and he refused, she angrily picked him up and put him in Time Out. When put in Time Out, the child beat his fist against the wall hard enough to dent the sheetrock. Before he punched a hole in the sheetrock, Mom let him out of Time Out. "But," she said to herself as her son fled from the Time-Out Chair, "just this once and never again." And at the time, she meant it.

A few evenings later, her son again would not go to bed as directed. So Mom again put her son in Time Out. "This time," she told herself, "he is not getting out until he is ready to comply and go to bed!"

Immediately, the boy started beating on the wall. He beat on the wall until his fist hurt, but his mother never wavered. When the boy realized that beating on the wall with his fist was not sufficient going to get him out of Time Out, he started banging his head against the wall. He beat his head against the wall until blood flowed down his face.

Horrified, the mother gathered her son in her arms. "It's okay. Mommy has you," she said reassuringly. The Coercive Cycle was not broken. It was strengthened.

> **KEY CONCEPT**
>
> The Coercive Cycle is incredibly difficult to break.

If parents are going to break the Coercive Cycle by making a frontal assault, there is only one way they can win. The parents have to dole out more punishment than the child is willing to absorb, and the parents have to punish the child harder than the child punishes them.

BREAKING THE COERCIVE CYCLE— A DIFFERENT APPROACH

There is another much more effective and positive way to break the Coercive Cycle. It involves making full use of the power of routines. The approach works because

- A routine makes the child's noncompliance his or her problem.
- A routine provides parents a vehicle for using supportive, nurturing techniques to guide their defiant child toward success.
- A routine gives defiant children a reason to develop self-calming techniques.

MAKING NONCOMPLIANCE THE CHILD'S PROBLEM

Despite your best intentions and efforts to support and help your child with her low-interest tasks, there will come a day when she flat out refuses. The adamancy of her refusal can be heard in her voice, seen in her eyes, and read on her face. There is no doubt about it. This is intentional defiance. Your child is looking for a confrontation, and she won't settle for anything less! Wanting to regain that old feeling of control, she is determined to engage you in a power struggle—one that she intends to win.

What are you to do?

Nothing! It is not your problem! There is no need for you to sternly issue a command. Nor do you have to threaten your child. You do not need to say, "Son, you have to take a bath, or else!" And when your child does not head toward the bathroom, you do not have to punish her into compliance.

A routine makes this destructive parent–child power struggle unnecessary. The routine does this by making the child's refusal to take a bath the child's problem. For example, Charlie, a 6-year-old, used to do pretty much what he wanted from after supper until bedtime, and even then he went to bed only when he was ready. So his parents implemented a routine. As usually happens, the routine in conjunction with the prevention techniques produced three weeks of good behavior and no incidents of noncompliance. However, then one evening it happened. Charlie adamantly refused to take a bath at 8:00 o'clock. At 8:25, which was only five minutes before this scheduled bedtime snack, Charlie stomped into the kitchen. "Where is my snack?" he demanded to know.

"What comes before the bedtime snack?" his mother asked. Charlie got the point, and he realized that if he did not take a bath, he was not going to get his bedtime snack. He can then take one of four possible courses of action.

> **KEY CONCEPT**
>
> A routine removes the necessity for parent-child power struggles.

POSSIBLE RESPONSES TO NOT GETTING THE PAYOFF

Possible Response 1: Ask for Help.   Charlie quickly saw that his mother was not going to get into a power struggle with him by trying to force him into the bathtub. However, he also saw that his mother was not preparing his bedtime snack. Seeing what was about to unfold, Charlie asked for help. But his appeal for help was not sweet, nor was it apologetic. It was sharp and demanding. "Well," he snapped, trying to make it appear as if the breakdown in the routine was his mother's fault, "Are you going to run my bath or not?"

Mrs. Williams was tempted to say, "I will help you, but not when you speak to me in that tone! If you want me to help you, make it sound nice and say please." But she didn't. Instead, Mrs. Williams realized that Charlie had just reached out for help in the best way that he knew how. Right now, the kid was struggling. His request, as sharp and as demanding as it sounded, was, nonetheless, a plea for help. In asking for help, Charlie had made a gigantic step. Recognizing that this was not the time to demand humility and contrition, Mrs. Williams made the perfect response. "You bet," she replied.

Possible Response 2: Get His Own Snack. When Charlie adamantly refused to take a bath that evening, Mrs. Williams waited for him to experience the natural consequence of that decision—no bedtime snack. But to her surprise, Charlie went into the kitchen and prepared himself a bedtime snack.

Instantly, Mrs. Williams realized that she had lost the battle that evening. But losing one battle did not mean the war was lost. It simply meant that Mrs. Williams needed to examine why the routine did not work that evening.

If Charlie went into the kitchen that evening and found a piece of cake in the refrigerator, Mrs. Williams knew what she needed to do. Thereafter, Mrs. Williams made sure that there were no convenient desserts, candy, or junk food in the house. Taking care of this, Mrs. Williams was once again in control of the payoff, thereby restoring the power of the routine.

However, if Charlie got out peanut butter, jelly, and bread that evening and made himself a sandwich, there was a different lesson to be learned. Mrs. Williams realized that she no longer had control over the payoff. She needed to find a new payoff following bath—one over which she had control. As it often is, the solution for regaining control was relatively simple. Charlie loved baked desserts. For example, he loved a slice of pie, a piece of cake, or a fresh-baked cookie. So at the beginning of each week, Mrs. Williams and Charlie planned out the "special" bedtime snack for each evening. Since Charlie could not bake and since he did not do the grocery shopping, Mrs. Williams again had control over the "special" payoff.

Possible Response 3: Have a Temper Tantrum. Upon seeing that he was not going to get his bedtime snack, Charlie had a temper tantrum. While the tantrum looked and sounded terrible, it wasn't. Charlie's temper tantrum was well-orchestrated theater. It was an act. Like most of his temper tantrums, its goal was to get Mom to give in. In this case, Charlie wanted his mother to prepare him a bedtime snack without his having to take a bath.

Knowing Charlie's intent, it was easy for Mrs. Williams to ignore Charlie's temper tantrum. So that Charlie did not have an audience for his performance, Mrs. Williams went into the living room and read a magazine.

Unfortunately, Charlie continued his temper tantrum until 8:50. By then, the window for having a bedtime snack had closed. It was time to move on. Charlie did not take a bath that evening, but neither did he get his bedtime snack.

When Charlie finally calmed down and appeared to be receptive to help, Mrs. Williams refocused Charlie's attention on the low-interest tasks that he had to complete in order to earn the next payoff. "Charlie," she said, "We will finish the dinosaur book tonight. Will you be ready for reading time?"

"I want my bedtime snack," Charlie whined, trying one last time to see if Mom might yet cave in. However, Mrs. Williams did not bite on Charlie's final attempt to engage her in a power struggle. Instead, she went to Charlie's communication board. Getting the brush teeth card, she silently handed it to him. As he reached for it, she said, "I'll get the dinosaur book and be waiting for you."

Possible Response 4: Have a Meltdown.   When Charlie saw that he was not going to get his bedtime snack, he had an emotional meltdown. An emotional meltdown has a few characteristics of a temper tantrum, but there are some important differences. When children have an emotional meltdown, they lose their capacity for behavior-regulating thought.[50] Quite literally, their brain short circuits. The brain stops sending signals to the frontal cortex—the area that sets goals and constructs plans to achieve those goals. Instead of planning, the brain's energy goes straight to the limbic system—the emotional part of the brain that responds to threats by either flight or fight.

When children have an emotional meltdown, it can be seen. Their eyes glaze over, giving them a non-seeing, disconnected look. Their face either flushes beat red or it blanches white. The muscles in their arms harden. Often, the blood vessels in their neck stand out like steel cords. Furthermore and more importantly, their actions become irrational and dangerous. When children are having an emotional meltdown, they are apt to unthinkingly destroy property or seriously hurt someone, even themselves.

Seeing these changes in Charlie, Mrs. Williams knew that soothing words, an appeal to logic, or stating a consequence for his behavior would not help. The behavior-regulating part of Charlie's brain was temporarily out of order. She had no choice but to physically control Charlie so that he did not destroy property or hurt anyone.

Physical Restraint

When children are having an emotional meltdown, parents often have to physically control them so that they do not destroy property or hurt anyone. The recommended physical restraint is a basket hold.

A basket hold is a safe way to restrain a child. Get behind your child and grab his left wrist with your right hand, and then grab his right wrist with your left hand. When both of Charlie's arms were grasped, Mrs. Williams pulled Charlie's arms tightly against his chest. Next and immediately, Mrs. Williams brought Charlie to the floor by taking away the child's legs as supports. She did this by pushing her knees against the back of Charlie's knees, causing his legs to fold. When Charlie's legs folded, gravity brought him to the floor.

Mrs. Williams and Charlie were now sitting on the floor. She was behind him, holding him. While in this position, Mrs. Williams protected her face in case Charlie made a backward head butt. She protected her face by turning her head to the side, pressing her cheek tight against the top of Charlie's shoulders.

Charlie struggled with all of his might to get out of the basket hold. When he couldn't, he was even more frustrated. "Let go of me. Let go of me right now!" he yelled at the top of his lungs.

"I will let go of you," Mrs. Williams calmly replied, "as soon as you can control yourself. You need to calm down." Gradually, Charlie stopped struggling. As he did, Mrs. Williams slightly loosened her hold on him. Her loosened grip told Charlie that as he de-escalated the struggle, his mother would respond in kind. When it seemed like Charlie's meltdown has passed, Mrs. Williams asked, "Are you calm?"

When Charlie said, "Yes" and also stopped struggling, Mrs. Williams further loosened her grip on his arms. But she was vigilant. She knew that Charlie's verbal assurance that he was calm often was a ruse. Upon being released, Charlie sometimes reverted to the behavior that necessitated the basket hold in the first place. So Mrs. Williams gradually released Charlie while remaining ready to reapply the basket hold at his first sign of aggression.

When putting your child in a basket hold, remain calm and unemotional. Convey your detachment by saying very little. Ideally, do not say any more than what has already been suggested.

DEMONSTRATE AND PRACTICE

If your child is apt to have an emotional meltdown, you need to pick a calm moment to explain to the child how you will respond when he has lost the capacity for self-control, and why you need to respond in this manner. Your explanation should be short and to the point. Try these words: "Sometimes you do things that could hurt people or could damage property. When you do, you need help. Let me show you how I will help you." Then demonstrate the basket hold while saying, "I am holding you like this to help you calm yourself. When you are calm, I will release your arms."

Initially, children resist being put in a basket hold. However, children usually come to accept the necessity of the basket hold. When they realize that a basket hold prevents them from hurting people or breaking property and keeps them safe, many children come to accept and even welcome being put in a basket hold.

TEACHING CHILDREN HOW TO GAIN SELF-CONTROL

If your child occasionally needs to be put in a basket hold, he or she needs to learn how to calm her- or himself before the emotional meltdown. You can teach your child how to calm himself or herself.

Randy, an 8-year-old boy, was a case in point. When Randy refused to help pick up his things during the family pickup time, he missed the payoff of being able to watch his favorite television program. In a fit of anger, Randy grabbed a cushion off of the couch and threw it at a lamp, breaking it. He then slammed his fist against the wall, punching a hole in the sheetrock. This was not a temper tantrum put on so that he could get his own way. His glazed-over eyes and blanched white face were his telltale signs of an emotional meltdown. Mr. McFarland knew that he had to put Randy in a basket hold to prevent further property destruction.

Randy Takes Control

That evening, just before bedtime, Mr. McFarland went in to Randy's bedroom to read to his son. "Randy," he said, fluffing up Randy's pillow. "I am wondering how you felt earlier this evening when it was necessary for us to use a basket hold."

"Oh, I don't know," Randy replied, trying to drop the conversation. "Just read."

"I'll read, but first I'd like us to discuss what happened. I'm wondering whether you would you like to find a way to avoid basket holds."

"Ya," Randy said lamely.

"So let's put our heads together. When you start to get upset, is there something you could do to keep that anger from spilling out?"

"What do you mean?"

"Well, when I start to get angry, I sit down in a chair and read a magazine. In a few minutes, I'm not even thinking about what made me angry. That's what works for me. What do you think would work for you?"

"I don't want to read nothin'. When I get angry, I'm too mad to sit and do anything!"

"You are doing a good job identifying what will not work for you. That is good thinking. And so what might work for you? Do you have any ideas?"

"No."

"Let's think about a place. Where in this house is the best place for you to calm yourself. Would you be more likely to be calm in the kitchen, the living room, or in your bedroom?"

"My bedroom."

"So when you are angry, the best place for you to go would be your room?"

"Yup!"

"And what would you do in your room?

"I'd get a pillow, and I'd punch it and punch it and punch it till I wasn't mad no more."

"Randy, it sounds like YOU have a good plan for getting your anger under control. You will go to your room and punch a pillow over and over and over until your anger is gone. That is an excellent plan. Do you want to try it?"

"Sure."

MAKE IT LEGAL

William Glasser developed this child-centered, problem-solving approach and presented it in his book *Reality Therapy*. Glasser maintained that the child's plan becomes more compelling when it is drafted into a formal-looking agreement, complete with signatures.[51] Accordingly, Mr. McFarland typed the following document:

Randy's Plan

The Problem: When I get angry, I sometimes throw things. One time I threw a cushion, and the cushion hit a lamp, knocking it over and breaking it. I am now paying for the lamp out of my allowance.

Calming Down: When I get angry, my plan is to go to my room. I will punch a pillow over and over until I am done being angry.

Help Wanted: It would help me if Mom or Dad asked me whether I need to go punch my pillow. But let me make the choice.

_____	_____
Randy McFarland	*Mark McFarland*
_____	_____
Mavis McFarland	*Date*

COMMITMENT

To help children take ownership of their plan, they need to tell other people about it. They should share their plan with at least three people. In addition to sharing his plan with Mom and Dad, Randy shared his plan with his third-grade teacher and with Mrs. Curl, an elderly lady who occasionally came into the house to provide child care. Mr. McFarland alerted these people that Randy wanted to share something important with them, thereby priming them to be good listeners.

ANTECEDENTS/TRIGGERS

Defiant children are incapable of recognizing the events that trigger their emotional meltdowns. They need a parent or caregiver to help them recognize when something happens that is going to cause them to have a meltdown.

This is yet another advantage of a routine. When a child is following a routine, one main thing causes a meltdown: not completing the low-interest tasks that are necessary to earn a payoff. However, the child does not have a meltdown upon losing every payoff, only some payoffs some of the time. Children show that they are about to lose it in different ways. Some bounce around, going from one thing to the next. Others get argumentative. A few withdraw. Whatever the sign is for your child, you will know. Upon seeing the conditions that precede an emotional meltdown, you must assist your child in implementing his or her plan.

In Randy's case, the trigger for his emotional meltdown was not getting his bedtime snack. But there was an even earlier antecedent. Randy took his first step toward an emotional meltdown as soon as he failed to complete a low-interest task that was necessary to earn his bedtime snack. Knowing this, Mr. and Mrs. McFarland saw how they could help Randy implement his self-calming plan long before his anger became so overwhelming that he had a meltdown. When they saw that Randy was not doing a low-interest task and that his anger was building, they could say, "Randy, would it help you to go punch your pillow for a while?"

> **KEY CONCEPT**
>
> Children who have emotional meltdowns need a parent or caregiver to help them recognize the antecedents for the meltdown so they can take preventive action.

ROLE-PLAY

When children attempt to change their behavior, they need to practice the new behavior. This calls for role-plays. When doing role-plays, each successive episode gets increasingly realistic until a point is reached that a role-play is hard to distinguish from the real thing. Role-plays are important for two reasons. First, they help the child practice the preventive actions, imprinting the visual, auditory, and other sensations into his or her mind and making the needed action a habit. Second, role-plays make it clear to the child that even though he or she made a mistake, there is a win-win outcome available.

Mr. McFarland did several role-plays with Randy. The first role-play was simple. On cue, Mr. McFarland said, "Randy, does your pillow need punching?" Smiling, Randy went to his room and punched his pillow. Next, Mr. McFarland had Randy not do a low-interest task and start to get angry. When the stage was set, Dad said, "Randy, does your pillow need punching?"

Finally, Mr. McFarland actually prompted Randy to not complete a low-interest task and then find out that he would not get his bedtime snack. As Randy pretended to have a meltdown, Dad asked, "Randy, does your pillow need punching?" As soon as Randy went to his room and punched the pillow a couple of times, Mr. McFarland said, "That was a great role-play Randy, now let's go do that last task so that you can have your bedtime snack."

SELF-CHARTING

When children chart the target behavior, it keeps the issue in the forefront of their mind, giving them mental practice in implementing their plan. Accordingly, Randy completed this self-charting document:

Following My Plan

Goal: When I get angry, I will go my room, lie on the bed, and punch my pillow.

Each evening I will complete this chart by placing an X in the appropriate boxes. I will do this chart for one week.

	Sun.	Mon.	Tues.	Wed.	Thurs.	Fri.	Sat.
Did not need the plan.							
Needed the plan and followed it.							
Needed the plan but did not follow it.							

A little bit of self-charting is good, but more is not better. The maximum benefit of self-charting is obtained in one week. That is the amount of time it takes for the child to commit the plan to memory and get some practice in using it. Once the child "knows" the plan, it is then a question of whether the plan will work. More charting is not needed to accomplish that. Furthermore, after a week self-charting becomes an action done with little thought and no reflection.

NO FAIL

There are times when the first plan, such as the one that Randy developed with help from his dad, does not work. When that happens, do not say or even imply that your child failed. Rather, the plan failed your child. If the plan fails, the parent says, "Hey, that plan was a good start. But it seems to need a little improvement. Let's figure out how we can make the plan better." Almost always, the child knows why the plan failed, and he or she can make good suggestions for revising the plan so that it will work.

KEY CONCEPT

If the child does not follow the plan, it is not the child who failed. Rather, the plan failed the child.

APPLICATIONS

1. Making defiance the child's problem: The child's failure to follow the routine is the child's problem only if you let it be. This means that you do not issue Alpha Commands or make ultimatums when the child is struggling to complete a low-interest task in his or her routine. To guard against issuing Alpha Commands and making ultimatums, complete the following exercise with two or more tasks for the first week that the routine is implemented.

Task the child refused to do	How I used the power of the routine
8:10 Clifford had not started his bath	I asked, "Clifford, what does your routine say?"
8:50 Rusty is not brushing his teeth	I asked, "Rusty, what comes before reading?"
8:45 Justin did not get his bath done	Justin did not get his snack
_____	_____
_____	_____

2. Being a helper: When your child struggles to complete a low-interest task, she is giving you an opportunity to be a helper. One of the ways you can help is by asking a question (as opposed to giving a directive) that helps your child focus on that task at hand. Offering a choice is good way to accomplish this. Examples are:

> Do you want to play with the duck in the bathtub or do you want to play with the boat?
>
> Do you want me to start your bath water?
>
> When it is time for your snack?

Child struggled with	I helped by asking
_____	_____
_____	_____
_____	_____

3. Is your child likely to display behavior that could threaten health, safety, or property?

_____ Yes _____ No

If yes, find a time when you and your child can have a short talk. During the talk, be frank but gentle. "Son, I see that when you get upset there is chance that you might do something that could hurt someone, or you might do something that could break property. We don't do that in our house. So let me show you how I will help you calm yourself." Then model the basket hold.

4. Helping the child calm him- or herself: Complete the following plan.

_____[name]_____'s Plan

Behavior of Concern: _____

Plan for Self-Calming: _____

Requested Assistance: _____

_____   _____   _____

(signed) [Parent]   [Child]   Date

   a. Type the plan.
   b. Get signatures.
   c. Help the child share his or her plan with at least three people.
   d. Using the chart on page 125, have the child self-chart his or her ability to follow the plan for one week.

5. If the child still has outbursts that threaten people's safety or property, the child did not fail. The plan failed. Write a new plan.

7

Rules and Tools

Households need rules. But the rules must make sense. History has repeatedly shown that people do not comply with rules that don't make sense to them. The Prohibition Act of 1920 was a case in point. Since most U.S. citizens felt they had a right to drink alcoholic beverages, the consumption of alcohol did not decrease after the passage of the Act; it increased.[52] Children respond similarly. They balk at rules that don't make sense. When developing rules for children, parents must resist the temptation to make an exhaustively long list. The expectation that more rules leads to better control is illusionary. Instead of resulting in better control, a long list of rules blurs the distinction between what would be nice and what is essential. And even worse, you end up exhausting yourself with meaningless battles.

Essential rules keep the household safe and functioning. That takes only three rules:

- People in the household do not physically hurt or threaten to hurt anyone, including themselves.
- People in the household cannot break or threaten to destroy anyone's property, including stealing or taking things.

- No one can do things that deprive other people of their basic right to enjoy their home.

The first two rules make sense to children. Mere toddlers instinctively understand that they should not hurt people. By the time they are preschoolers, children realize that they should not take or break other people's things. The third rule is more difficult for children to understand. It amounts to this: When people live together in a home, there is a basic quality of life that each family member can expect. For example, a family member has the right to expect a decent night's sleep. A 5-year-old cannot wander around the house at two in the morning, forcing Mom to get up and supervise him. Family members have a right to expect that they can enjoy a meal without someone having a temper tantrum at the table and, in the process, flipping over the mashed potatoes. No one should be startled out of their sleep at three in the morning by a 12-year-old playing loud music. While all of the basic rights that family members can expect are too many to list, they fit into phrase that is used to describe gray situations: It might be hard to describe, but you know it when you see it.

However, these three little rules come with one big caveat. The rules apply to everyone in the family. Jillian cannot hit Mom, and Mom cannot hit Jillian.

In addition to having rules that make sense, there must be a compelling reason to follow them. In other words, when someone does not follow a rule, something must happen. But what?

IN SEARCH OF THE RIGHT CONSEQUENCE

PUNISHMENT

When children do not follow a rule, the first thought that comes to mind is that they should be punished. In its behaviorist context, punishment means that the parent should do something to the child that decreases the likelihood that the child will break the rule again.[53] But to you and me, punishment has a straightforward meaning. Punishment means doing something to the child so that he regrets—really regrets—what he did, and he will not do that bad thing again for fear of being punished.

When we think of punishment, spanking immediately comes to mind. Indeed, spanking is such a common method of disciplining children that there is an adage promoting its use: Spare the rod and spoil the child. Many people, including a few behavioral experts,[54] believe in spanking.

Overcorrection is another form of punishment.[55] Overcorrection means that when a child does something wrong, the child is punished by having to do the correct action over and over, again and again. The intent of Overcorrection is not to teach the child a new skill. Rather, the intent is to sufficiently humiliate the child so that she never does it again. For example, a teacher catches a student running down the stairs at school, and the student is made to walk up and down the stairs twenty-five times.

There is also Response Cost.[56] In order to use Response Cost, there has to be an incentive in place prior to the child's violating the rule. For example, at the beginning of the week the teacher announces that students who earn 20 points can watch a video on Friday afternoon. One point is awarded for every homework assignment turned in on time, but two points are taken away for any homework assignment that is not turned in on time. Response Cost is a reward system with a barb. The barb is that when the child fails to do the desired behavior, tokens are taken away. Taking away tokens is what makes Response Cost a punishment. It hurts to lose tokens, and it usually makes defiant children angry—very angry.

Time Out is a commonly used and widely recommended method of punishing children.[57] When using Time Out, the parents make the child go someplace, usually a chair facing the corner, and stay there for a period of time and until certain conditions are met. The guideline is that the child sits in the Time Out chair one minute for every year of age.[58] So a 6-year-old child would sit in the Time Out chair for six minutes, while a 10-year-old chair would sit in the Time Out chair for ten minutes. Furthermore, the noncompliant child stays in the chair for that predetermined amount of time **and** until she is ready to comply with her parent's directive.

The Case for Punishment.   Punishment is often an effective way to immediately get a behavior to terminate. Furthermore, as long as the punisher is present (meaning, in this case, the parent) the child is not likely to engage in that bad behavior. Punishment is particularly good as a knee-jerk response to an unpredicted and unexpected bad behavior. For example, a toddler is reaching out toward a hot stove burner, and his mother quickly gives him a swat on the behind and says, "No!" The child immediately pulls his hand back and goes crying out of the kitchen. At least he did not burn his hand.

The Case Against Punishment.   There are many reasons why parents should not punish children. For starters, punishing a child teaches her what she shouldn't do, but it does absolutely nothing to teach the child the right thing to do. Punishment would be okay if the main job of parenting were to control children's behavior until they reach the age of 18 and are ready, so to speak, to leave the house. But parenting is not about stopping children from doing bad things. Parenting is about teaching children how to have a rewarding productive life. That is one big task, and punishment does not do anything to help parents accomplish that task.

The main case against using punishment is that punishing defiant children often makes them more aggressive. Furthermore, in order to punish children, parents have to be a big mean enforcer. Consider the harshest form of punishment—spanking. Not many defiant children willingly submit to be spanked; in fact, they often do everything they can to resist being spanked, often hitting, kicking, and biting. When the child resists spanking, it becomes a parent–child fight—one that the parent, even with superior strength and size, might not win.

Consider Overcorrection. A child was supposed to do homework for thirty minutes, but he didn't. So the parent said, "Since you did not do any homework for the entire thirty minutes, you will do it for an hour and a half. Hearing this, the defiant child goes up to his room and hides under his bed. What is the parent going to do? In order to enforce Overcorrection, the parent has to reach under the bed, grab the child by the leg and pull him kicking and screaming our from under the bed. That is only the start of it. The parent then has to get the child to his study area and physically force him to stay there for ninety minutes.

Response Cost suffers the same problem. How willingly does a defiant child surrender tokens that it took him two days to earn? Response Cost has an additional shortcoming. Let's say that the parents use Response Cost to get Cassie to pick up her bedroom every evening. Accordingly, they give Cassie a token every evening that she picks up her room, but they take away two tokens if Cassie does not pick up her room. If Cassie has seven tokens by Sunday afternoon, she can go to the Sunday afternoon movie. Excited by the anticipated reward, Cassie finds a friend who will go with her to the movie. Thus motivated, Cassie picks up her room for three consecutive evenings. But Wednesday, she does not. So her parents take away two tokens. Cassie instantly realizes that she will not be able to go to the Sunday movie with her friend, and she is furious. What are the chances that Cassie will pick up her room for the rest of the week?

Time Out is intended to be a mild punishment, and it is if the child willingly goes to Time Out. However, many defiant children do not go willingly to Time Out. What is a parent to do then? Again, Time Out will only be effective if the parent is the ultimate enforcer. So the parent grabs the child and tries to pull him to the Time Out chair. The child fights back, hitting and kicking. Frustrated and angry, many parents then spank the child. But their mild spanks don't get the child to go to Time Out. So the parent spanks the child hard—really hard. Suddenly, Time Out, which was intended to be a very mild punishment, is verging on physical abuse.

The final problem with using punishment to control a child's bad behavior is that in order to get any form of punishment to work, parents almost always end up violating the very rule they set out to enforce; namely, *people in this house do not physically hurt anyone.* When the parents' use of punishment violates this rule, children quickly learn the lesson that was just taught: Big people can use aggression against little people.

A BRIEF HISTORY OF PUNISHMENT

Using punishment to control behavior has a long history. In the era known as the Enlightenment (1600–1700), people who would now be diagnosed with schizophrenia were thought to be possessed by the devil.[59] They were severely and horribly punished in the belief that the punishment would literally drive the devil out of them. Vestiges of that mentality still survive when we teasingly say to an impish, full of vinegar child, "You are full of the devil today."

Punishing people with other handicapping conditions in an attempt to control their behavior did not go out with the dark ages. Only four decades ago, punishment was commonly used in attempts to change the behavior of people with mental retardation, particularly those individuals unfortunate enough to be placed in state-run institutions.[60] However, beginning in the late 1960s, punishment was less and less used to control the behavior of people with mental retardation. Today, behavior programming designed to punish people with mental handicaps is the unacceptable exception. As a result, people who were once tethered by straps to granite pillars in the day rooms of mental institutions now live happily in their own supervised apartments and make money working in what are called work enclaves or supported employment.

Next in line for punishment were persons with autism. Only a few decades ago, the most widely advocated treatment for persons with autism was to punish them for their autistic-like behaviors. Fortunately, many therapists are now realizing that people with autism do not decrease their autistic-like behaviors when punished. Instead, children with autism learn best and behave better when provided unique specific structure that enables them to organize and make sense of their world.[61]

Children with Oppositional Defiant Disorder are among the last remaining behaviorally challenged people for whom punishment is deemed good therapeutic treatment. To be candid, it is tempting to punish defiant children. They spit in your face, they tip over desks, they curse you, and they adamantly, obstinately, and defiantly refuse to comply with even the most basic reasonable directives. It just feels good to punish them. After all, there are times when we all feel that a particular defiant child really has it coming!

However, I refuse. I refuse to punish defiant children because history says that it is not the right approach. Punishment was not the answer for people with schizophrenia. Punishment was not the answer for helping people with mental retardation, and punishment was not the right approach for helping children with autism. Why would punishment be the answer for children with Oppositional Defiant Disorder? But the reasons that I refuse to punish defiant children are more personal. I refuse to punish children when I think of how one defiant child, Mike, responded when he was punished.

Getting Even

Years ago, I consulted weekly at an agency that served children with a variety of disabilities. Late one afternoon, I was in my office typing a report. A 15-year-old boy, Mike, came into the room to do his daily chore of sweeping the floor. Mike was not one of my patients, but I knew him by his well-earned reputation. Mike had Oppositional Defiant Disorder. If Mike did not like someone, he would not do anything that person asked, and if pushed he would become aggressive. His selective defiance and targeted aggression was why Mike was at our residential treatment program.

While I typed my report, Mike started to sweep behind my chair. Taking a break from his sweeping, he said, "I'm gonna phone Mary tonight."

Knowing that Mary was his case manager, I said, "That will be nice, Mike. Mary will appreciate hearing from you." Mike gave me a confused look. Again, he said, "I am gonna phone Mary tonight." Seeing that I was missing something, I said, "And what are you going to say to Mary?"

"Nothing!" Mike said empathetically.

"Nothing?"

"Nope. When she answers the phone, she is not going to hear nothin'."

"And why silence?"

"It will be two o'clock in the morning. That is the time I'm gonna set my alarm for."

"And why are you going to do that to Mary?" I asked.

"Cuz last Monday I didn't make my bed and she told me that I couldn't go to the movie this weekend. So I am getting even with her. Yesterday I let the air out of her car tires. Tonight I am phoning her at two in the morning. Tomorrow I'm gonna put a snake in her desk drawer. Then I'll be even."

Mike taught me that defiant children resent being punished, and when defiant children are punished, they set out to get even.

> ### KEY CONCEPT
> Punishing children over time often makes them more defiant.

I Pray to God

Every time that I am tempted to punish a defiant child, I think of Calvin. Calvin was a 10-year-old boy. By appearance, Calvin was intelligent, good looking, and, at a few rare moments, sweet. But he had many behavior problems, his primary diagnosis being Oppositional Defiant Disorder.

I first met Calvin (rather, Calvin was first brought to my attention) when he was placed in a residential treatment program. He
seemed to be incorrigibly defiant. Told to do even the simplest
things, Calvin adamantly refused. If directed to fold five articles of
his freshly washed clothing, Calvin would throw the clothes all over
his room. It then took a lot of staff prompting, prodding, and
threatening a major consequence before, some two and half hours
later, he finally complied. Even the seasoned staff at the treatment
facility developed a strong dislike for Calvin. No wonder—he
fought them at every turn. The more they tried to force Calvin to
comply, the more defiant and noncompliant Calvin became. As one
staff put it, "I am willing to bet that if I told Calvin he had to eat
his ice cream, he would throw it in the garbage can."

However, there was another, seldom seen, side of Calvin. When
Calvin was in his room at the end of the day and the stresses and
difficulties of the day were behind him, he became a different child.
I liked to think that he became the real Calvin. One such evening,
after reading to him from a chapter book, I tucked him into bed
and started to leave. "Can I talk to you a minute?" he asked.
Something in his voice told me that he was not stalling for time. He
really wanted to talk, and it was important to him.

"Sure. What is it that you want to talk about, Calvin?"

"Every night just before I go to sleep, I pray to God. I ask God to
help me be good the next day. When the next day starts, I get out of
bed thinking that God answered my prayers and I will be good.
Then the day starts. Things happen, and before I know it I am bad."
He paused, as if thinking about something and wondering whether
he should say it. After a time, he did. "Do you think if I keep pray-
ing to God, he will answer my prayers, and one day I will be good?"

I did not interpret Calvin to be asking to be punished so he could
be good. I understood him to be asking his caregivers, to determine
the structure, to develop the supports, and to provide the timely
affirmations that he needed in order to be good.

It is both my conviction and my experience that there is a desire to be
good within each and every oppositional defiant child. But if the caregiver

punishes the child and uses other coercive measures to get the defiant child to comply with directives and requests, no one, possibly not even the child, ever sees this deep-seated desire to be good. This desire to be good only awakens within a defiant child when he or she feels emotionally and physically safe in the caregiver's presence, and when he or she feels that despite all of the problems he or she has caused, you continue to value, to believe in, and to want to help him or her.

LOGICAL CONSEQUENCES

Parents are reluctant to give up punishment as a tool for controlling their child's behavior because they believe that no punishment means no discipline. It doesn't. You can stop punishing your child because there is a far better way to enforce the three cardinal rules, a way that results in:

- Better discipline.
- A strengthened parent–child bond.
- An empowered, more capable child.

This better way is based on the principle of logical consequences.

The principle of logical consequences says that when a child does something that could hurt people, could damage property, or threatens to disrupt the household, the child loses a privilege(s).[62] But children don't lose a privilege as a punishment. Rather, children lose privileges to the extent necessary to prevent them from hurting people, from breaking things, or from denying other people the right to enjoy their home. It often happens that the child feels badly about losing the privilege. For example, an 8-year-old boy has a friend over to play. After fifteen minutes, they start to fight. The most obvious logical consequence is that the friend needs to go home. Of course, the boy feels bad. That is unfortunate, but the friend was not taken home in an effort to make the child feel bad; the friend was sent home so that no one got hurt. If the child protests the logical consequence, it would perfectly okay (in fact, it would be outstanding) to say, "The issue here is that no one gets hurt. Can you think of another solution that absolutely guarantees that there will be no fighting? If you can, that is what we will do."

As previously mentioned, children inherently understand they cannot hurt people, break things, or damage property. With a little bit of explanation, they can understand that it is not permissible to deny other people their right to enjoy their home. So even defiant children typically accept and understand when a parent removes a privilege in order to maintain these things.

> **KEY CONCEPT**
>
> When a logical consequence is imposed and child loses a privilege, the child may well feel bad about the loss of the privilege. But that is beside the point. The important point is that losing the privilege protected or restored other people's rights.

The difference between a logical consequence and punishment is subtle and hard to discern. An example will make the distinction clearer. It's lunchtime at the Woodrow Wilson Elementary School. Mr. Burke, the fourth-grade teacher, told his students to line up at the door. As the students stood at the door and waited for Mr. Burke's signal to exit the classroom, one of the students became impatient. Breaking out of line, Paul slipped out the door. Once in the hall, Paul did not want Mr. Burke to see him, so he ran down the hall. As he sped pass the classroom doors, Paul impulsively rapped on each one.

When Mr. Burke caught up with Paul in the lunchroom, Mr. Burke could have said, "Paul, since you ran down the hall, you will not have recess for the rest of the week!"

Going out for recess is a privilege, but withholding recess from Paul because he ran down the hall would not have been a logical consequence. Withholding recess would have been punishment. It would be punishment because it would have been imposed in order to make Paul feel so bad that he would never again run down the hall. Staying in from recess is not a logical consequence in this situation because losing that privilege does nothing to protect a kindergarten student from being run over the next time Paul runs down the hall, and it does not to prevent Paul from disrupting every classroom he runs by on his mad dash to lunch.

Instead of punishing Paul, Mr. Burke gave him a logical consequence. "Paul," Mr. Burke said, "I see that it is hard for you to walk down the hall to lunch. So tomorrow, you will need to remain in your desk while the others line up for lunch (losing a privilege). As soon as they are gone, you can walk with me to the lunchroom" (thus protecting students' safety and their right to learn without being disturbed).

HELPING CHILDREN UNDERSTAND WHY

Imposing a logical consequence creates an opportunity for you to teach your child important social skills and understandings. In other words, the child can benefit from his mistake. To explain how this happens, again consider the example of Paul running down the hall. When Paul and his teacher met on Friday, Mr. Burke asked, "Paul, why do think the school has a rule against running in the hall?" Mr. Burke was sure of two things: (1) Paul had never thought about it, and (2) he could figure it out.

"They don't want anyone to get hurt? Like what if a little kindergarten student stepped out of a door while I was running by? Why, I'd run right over him. And running makes a lot of noise when others kids are studying."

"That's exactly right, Paul! That is why the school has a rule against running in the hall. You have a good head on your shoulders. I knew you could figure it out."

Clearly, Mr. Burke is a skilled teacher who knows how to expertly guide an errant child's social development. The key to facilitating your child's special development is to **not tell** the child why his or her actions were unacceptable. **Ask.** In order to do that, two things are required.

1. Your child must see you as being there to help and support, as opposed to punishing.
2. When your child views you in that role, you simply ask, just as Mr. Burke did, "Why do you think. . . ?"

HELPING CHILDREN DEVELOP "CAN DO" PLANS

By using logical consequences, you are in a position to teach your child the skills she needs in order to regain a temporarily lost privilege. Returning to the example, Mr. Burke helped Paul develop a "can do" plan. He said, "Paul, I know it is difficult for you to walk in the hall. So for the next couple of days, I want you to think about what you can do in order to walk. If you come up with any ideas, I will have some time Friday to listen to them. If it's a good idea and we think it might work, you can then rejoin the class when they walk to lunch. Would you like to do that?"

"Sure," Paul replied, pleased to learn that he could regain the privilege of walking with the rest of the class.

When they met Friday, Mr. Burke said, "So tell me, Paul, what ideas have you come up with so that you can remember to walk in the hall?"

"I won't run any more, I promise," Paul replied in all sincerity. He meant every word of his vow not to run in the hall again. However, Paul's vow was a stop plan. Stop plans don't work.[63] Stop plans don't work because children seldom set out to intentionally do bad things. Rather, when impulsive children are confronted by a compelling array of events and situations, bad things just seem to happen.

KEY CONCEPT

Stop plans don't work.

In Paul's case, he did not run down the hall because he wanted to maliciously put other children's safety at risk, nor did he derive satisfaction out of disrupting other students. Paul probably ran down the hall because he was hungry. He likely ran down the hall because he had been sitting quietly at his desk for an hour, which was about as long as he could stand it. He possibly ran down the hall because he looked out the classroom door and saw that the other fourth-grade class was already headed for the lunchroom. All of these things impinged on him at once, and their combined force was just too compelling. So Paul impulsively stepped out the door. Once out the classroom door, Paul knew he had done the wrong thing. But it was too late. So he ran down the hall, hoping that he could make it to the lunchroom without Mr. Burke noticing that he was missing.

Like Paul, most defiant children have no insight into why they do unacceptable things. And having no insight into why they did something, they have no ability to identify the conditions that prompt that behavior. Since the child cannot recognize the conditions that set off the behavior, the conditions control defiant children.

The solution is to help the defiant child recognize the conditions that, if unchecked, compel him or her to impulsively do stupid things. Mr. Burke gave Paul this needed help.

> **KEY CONCEPT**
>
> Children do not have insight into why they sometimes behave in unacceptable ways.

"Paul," Mr. Burke asked, "who is the one boy in the class who is certain to never run down the hall?

"Oh, that's easy. It would be Neil. He's too fat to run."

"Yes, Neil is not one to move very fast. And how do you get along with Neil?"

"Fine."

"So if you picked one student to always stand behind while you are standing in line for lunch, would it be Neil?"

"Ya. I like him."

"I notice that when you stand in the lunch line, your hands are busy touching things and your arms are always in motion. It seems to me that it is your busy arms that get your legs going, and once those legs get going, you forget to walk. So I was wondering what you could do to keep your arms still?"

"I can't think of anything," Paul replied, looking genuinely puzzled.

"Stand right in front of me." Paul did so. "Now look at your pants. What part of your pants are your hands next to?

"My pockets?"

"Yes! Your hands are right next to your pockets. Put your hands in your pockets." Paul did this. "Now swing your arms."

"I can't." Paul replied.

"Does that give you an idea?"

"You mean maybe I could put my hands in my pockets?" Paul asked.

"Would putting your hands in your pockets keep your arms from swinging?" Mr. Burke asked.

"Ya!" Paul replied, seemingly surprised at the potential of this simple idea.

"Good. Now I think you have a plan. Let's review it. When it is lunch time, who are you going line up behind?"

"Neil."

"And you are going to always stay behind him, right?"

"Right!" Paul replied, smiling at the idea that this plan was coming together.

"And where are you going to put your hands?"

"In my pockets."

"Do you think we should try that plan?

"Ya."

"Okay, we will. I want you to write out those three things that you will do to help you walk to lunch instead of run. When you have written out those three things you will do, show me. We will both sign it. As soon as we sign it, we will try it. We could start this noon if we are ready."

Imposing a logical consequence created an opportunity for Mr. Burke to help Paul gain insight as to why running down the hall was not acceptable. The logical consequence also allowed Mr. Burke to help Paul develop a "can do" plan for creating the new conditions that would anchor him in the lunch line and counter the conditions that compelled Paul to run in the hall. A logical consequence had one additional benefit, and that benefit was huge. In helping Paul develop a "can do" plan so that he could regain the privilege of walking with his classmates, Mr. Burke had numerous opportunities to affirm Paul, thereby strengthening his relationship with Paul.

FINDING A GOOD LOGICAL CONSEQUENCE

Sometimes it is difficult to pick the right logical consequence. Some guidelines will help:

- A logical consequence is the loss of a privilege, it is not a pound of flesh.
- When the logical consequence is imposed, the resultant loss of privileges protects people, property, and basic rights.
- The loss of the privilege is restored when the caregiver helps the child develop a "can do" plan.

One of the parents in our parent-training groups used these three guidelines to develop a good logical consequence to deal with her daughter's life-threatening behavior. The problem was that the 5-year-old daughter slipped out of the house when Mom was not looking. It happened like this: Sarah was finished with half-day kindergarten at noon. When she came home, she ate lunch and then played for about an hour while her mother,

Melinda, did office work from her computer. At this time, Sarah was expected to play in the house. But sometimes Sarah didn't play in the house. Every now and then, Sarah slipped out the door and wandered down the street, going toward whatever caught her attention. One day Melinda suddenly noticed that the house was quiet, too quiet. Then she called for her daughter, but Sarah did not answer. She was gone. Frantic, Sandy went looking for her daughter. When Mom found her, Sarah was at the end of the block, teasing a big dog tethered to a chain.

Clearly, wandering out of the house put Sarah in danger. A logical consequence was needed. Sarah needed to lose a privilege so that she could not continue wandering out of the house and putting her life in danger. Melinda decided that a good logical consequence would be to take away Sarah's privilege of wearing shoes in the house. So when Sarah got home from kindergarten each day, Mom put Sarah's shoes on the top shelf in the bedroom closet. It worked. Without shoes, Sarah no longer wandered out of the house.

Restitution is also a logical consequence. If you break it, you pay for it, at least the child pays for the broken or damaged item within his or her age-appropriate ability to do so. For example, the child lashes out, knocking dad's glasses off and breaking a lens. The child needs to at least partially compensate for the expense of getting a new lens. If the child does not have any money, she probably needs to do an extra household chore for a period of time.

OTHER EXAMPLES

Initially, it is difficult to find a consequence for a behavior that is not a punishment but is a good logical consequence. Some examples will help:

Behavior	Logical Consequence
Throwing food at the table	Eat at a separate table in another room.
Breaking the glass in a picture	Perform extra chores to help pay for new glass.
Hour play time with a friend turns into a fight	Shorten the play time to 30 minutes.

RESTORING THE PRIVILEGE

A logical consequence has another huge advantage over punishment. The advantage is that you and your child can work together to find a way that the privilege possibly can be restored, usually by increasing the structure or teaching the child new skills.

Helping your child regain the privilege accomplishes three things. First, it gives your child the incentive needed to learn new skills, often furthering the child's social maturity. Second, as the child participates in the "think session" to regain the privilege, you are presented with numerous opportunities to praise and value your child. Third, helping the child regain the privilege allows you to strengthen that critical parent-child bond.

CONCLUSION

Parents must set limits for children and expect compliance. If the child does not adhere to any one of those limits, there absolutely has to be a consequence. The typical and easiest consequence is to punish the child, and punish him or her so severely he or she will never do it again. However, parenting is not about controlling cildren. Parenting is about teaching children the skills they need in many areas, including behavior. So it is time to move beyond punishment. By using logical consequences, parents can both consequent unacceptable behaviors and simultaneously teach the child how to behave appropriately.

APPLICATIONS

1. What behaviors does your child frequently display that you consider unacceptable, and when you observe those behaviors being displayed, how to do you typically respond?

   Behavior   **Typical Response**

   _____   ____ Ignore   ____ Time Out
                            ____ Say, "Stop That"   ____ Spank

   _____   ____ Ignore   ____ Time Out
                            ____ Say, "Stop That"   ____ Spank

   _____   ____ Ignore   ____ Time Out
                            ____ Say, "Stop That"   ____ Spank

2. From the above list, identify those behaviors that could hurt someone, could damage property, or impose on people's basic rights.

   _____   _____   _____

3. The behaviors listed above need a Logical Consequence. What would be a good Logical Consequence for those actions?

   Behavior   **Logical Consequence**

   _____   _____

   _____   _____

   _____   _____

4. Set aside a time to have a discussion with your child regarding any behaviors listed under item 3. By asking questions, try to get

the child to understand why those behaviors are not allowable. Then explain the logical consequence (loss of privilege) that will happen if those behaviors are observed.

5. If your child is frequently displaying behaviors that could hurt someone or could damage property, the child presumably has a skill deficit or lacks an important understanding or value. Consider how you are going to help the child acquire the missing skill or gain necessary understanding/values. Please understand that such learning may take time. It might be several months before the child has acquired the necessary skill or obtained the level of understanding necessary to exercise that privilege. Since this is an extensive and time-consuming task, select the child's most disturbing behavior, and start there.

Behavior   Learning Activity

_____   _____

_____   _____

_____   _____

Part III

PLANNING FOR SUCCESS IN THE COMMUNITY

It is tempting to believe that defiant children have behavior problems and temper tantrums only at home, and when they go to school or elsewhere in the community they behave perfectly. That is rarely the case. With few exceptions, a child who is noncompliant and defiant at home is noncompliant and defiant at school and in the community.

Therefore, parents must help their defiant children be successful in school and in other places in the community by doing two things. First, parents should be candid about their children's behavior problems with the adults who will be supervising her. Second, parents of defiant children need to work with adults who will be supervising their defiant children to help those adults develop the structure and the support their child needs to be successful at school and other places within the community. The next two chapters will give you guidance and suggestions for doing that.

8

Going to School

It is tempting for parents of defiant children to send them off to school and hope for the best. Why not? School is a new environment. School is exciting. There is much to learn in school. There are new children to play with. Moreover, teachers are good at helping children. They help children learn new information and also help children learn how to behave in the classroom and on the playground.

This is wishful thinking. In truth, school is demanding. At school, children have to do page after page of deskwork. At school, children have to sit quietly at their desk. At school, children have to listen attentively while the teacher explains new and difficult concepts. At school, children have to do what the teacher says: "Raise your hand, take your seat, get out your reading book." As if that isn't enough, at school children have to be polite and respectful from the moment they walk onto school grounds in the morning until they go home late in the afternoon. School is work, and it is particularly hard work for children with challenging behaviors. They need your help.

Start by meeting with the school principal—the school's instructional leader. Ideally, this visit happens in early May. In May, the principal is preparing each teacher's class roster for the next school year. Class rosters are prepared with two objectives in mind. One objective is to keep the classes balanced so that each teacher has a comparable workload. The teachers at each grade level should have about the same number of girls and boys, the same number of academically advanced students, the same number of academically challenged students, and the same number of behaviorally challenged students. The principal's second objective is to place students with special needs with the "right" teacher.

Your purpose in visiting the principal is to share information about your child so the administrator can place your child with the right teacher. Be candid. If the principal knows that your child has challenging behaviors and the nature of those problems, the administrator is better able to match your child's needs with a particular teacher's skills and abilities. Behaviorally challenged children need a teacher who is unflappable and organized and who will value them. Such teachers exist. They are working in every school. By telling the principal about your child's needs, your child has a better chance of being placed with such a teacher.

> **KEY CONCEPT**
>
> Take the initiative by meeting with the principal prior to the start of the school year.

The next person you need to visit with is the classroom teacher. Ideally, you will visit with the teacher just before school starts in the fall. Teachers come into school about a week before the students arrive. They come for in-service training and to get their classrooms ready. Given notice, the teacher will meet with you at this time. If not, the educator will arrange for you to meet during the first week of school.

The purpose of your meeting with the teacher is to share information about your child that will help the educator address your child's educational and behavioral needs. Again, you want to be candid about your child's challenging behavior as well as any learning problems. But don't fail to mention your child's strengths, accomplishments, and interests.

> **KEY CONCEPT**
>
> It is important to meet with your child's teacher during the first week of school.

The second purpose of your meeting with the teacher is to get involved with the school. Getting involved with the school is easy. Schools appreciate all of the help they can get, especially when it is free. You might volunteer to read to children, to provide additional supervision on field trips, to bring cookies to fund-raising bake sales, and so on. By being in the building, you will be noticed and your contributions will be noted. Teachers are more apt to go the extra mile to help your child if you have helped the school.

> **KEY CONCEPT**
>
> Make "their" school "your" school by volunteering and/or joining the parent–teacher association. Definitely attend all parent–teacher conferences.

You also want to find out when and where the school's parent–teacher association meets. These meetings are open to all parents who have a child attending that particular school. Go!

There are parent–teacher conferences at specific times during the academic year that are listed on the school calendar. Get a copy of the school calendar and use it as a reminder. During the parent–teacher conference, the teacher meets individually and privately with the parents of each student. The teacher will tell you about your child's academic progress and adjustment at school. If the teacher has concerns, these can be discussed. Parent–teacher conferences are not a one-way flow of information. You have important information that will help the teacher better understand how to help your child.

These preventive measures will help your child do better both academically and behaviorally in school. However, the preventive measures might not be sufficient. If that is the case, more is needed.

GETTING ADDITIONAL SERVICES

Many children with chronic behavior problems cannot be successful in the regular classroom unless they receive additional services. However, additional services cost the school district money. Additional services are offered only if it has been determined that all interventions available to the classroom teacher have been tried but were not successful.

At one of your parent–teacher conferences, the teacher may ask whether you are interested in exploring whether your child qualifies for additional services. There are three ways or routes for your child to get additional services and accommodations to meet his or her educational needs.

ROUTE 1: SPECIAL EDUCATION SERVICES FOR STUDENTS WHO ARE EMOTIONALLY DISTURBED

Special education services are an array of services, specialists, accommodations, and programming. You can think of accessing these services as getting a referral from your family doctor to a team of specialists.

Getting Special Education Services. The road to special education services begins with a Request for Evaluation. Someone from the school will assist you with the process of completing the Request for Evaluation. Among other things, the Request for Evaluation lists the assessments that will be done to determine whether your child qualifies for services, and it will identify the school personnel who will be completing each assessment. If you agree with the information on the form, you acknowledge your consent to the evaluation by signing and dating the form. The comprehensive evaluation is done at no cost to you, the parent. At this time, you will, as is required by federal law, be given a copy of the Parent Procedure Safeguards, known in some schools at the Parent's Rights Handbook.

Parent/Child Rights. In 1975, Congress passed and the President signed Public Law 94-142—The Education of Handicapped Children Act.[64] Since then, the Act has been revised, reissued, and even renamed several times. It is now known as the Individuals with Disabilities Education Improvement Act (IDEA). The most recent revision to IDEA was made in 2004 and, after considerable review and input, was issued on October 13, 2006.[65] The fine print has changed, but the spirit of the legislation remains the same. IDEA says the school must provide a free and appropriate education for students with disabilities. Among the types of disabilities specified by IDEA, the federal legislation says that schools must provide a free and appropriate education to students who have an emotional disturbance

(ED). Some defiant children have such severe behavior problems that they meet the criteria established by IDEA as having an emotional disturbance.

> **KEY CONCEPT**
>
> Schools have a legal obligation to provide extra services and accommodations for children who have an emotional disturbance.

The Evaluation.   In order for your child to be considered for special services, you have to have him or her evaluated. Immediately, you wonder whether you should have your child evaluated to determine whether he or she has an emotional disturbance (ED). In our opinion, the answer is an unqualified yes. The evaluation is not as "psychologically" revealing as you might fear. No one is going to be looking for hidden psychic demons, subconscious perverse thoughts, or dark family secrets. The evaluation consists of collecting numbers and measures on your child to compare with the numbers obtained for other children of your child's same age, same grade, and gender. Since you are at this part of the process, someone from the school will discuss with you every test that will be administered and each formal classroom observation that will be made and why those assessments are both useful and important. The school also will tell you who will do each assessment. If you do not want a particular test administered, the school will listen to your concerns and almost certainly accede to them. The bottom line is that your written consent is necessary for the school to initiate the evaluation.

The testing does not put undue pressure on your child. In fact, children enjoy the attention and affirmation that skilled evaluators give them for working hard and doing their best. Most important, you and the child's teacher will learn useful information about your child's academic skills, ability, and emotional adjustment.

When you sign the Request for Evaluation and hand it to a school employee, you set the wheels turning. By federal law, the school has sixty calendar days to complete the evaluation and hold an Assessment Results or Eligibility Meeting. If the child is found to be eligible for special education services, the school district then has thirty additional calendar days to determine exactly what services will be provided and to start providing those services.

The Eligibility Meeting.   When the evaluators have completed their assessments, you will be notified as to the date of the meeting. The purpose of the meeting is to review the assessment data and decide whether it supports qualifying the child for special education services. When the assessment data has been presented, the facilitator guides the group toward determining whether your child qualifies for special education services. Let's say that the answer is yes.

The Disability Category.   If the team determines that the child qualifies for services under the disability category of having an Emotional Disturbance, some parents suddenly bring the road to special education to a dead end. They find the label—an emotional disturbance—offensive. They do not want "everyone," or even anyone, thinking that their child has an emotional disturbance.

Their concerns are understandable. However, no label means no services. Furthermore, the child's behavior is what it is. The label does not make the child's behavior worse, and not having the label does not make the child's behavior better.

> **KEY CONCEPT**
>
> The ED label is necessary to get your child special services.

Developing an Educational Plan.   If the evaluation results indicate that your child meets the criteria for having an emotional disturbance, a second meeting is scheduled or, time permitting, the current meeting moves to the next agenda item—determining what programming is needed to meet the child's needs. This process is called developing the student's Individualized Educational Plan, or IEP, as educators call it.

Parent's Role.   You are the most important person at the meeting! Your importance is underscored by federal statute. By law, no meeting, regardless of what it might be called, may be held to determine whether your child qualifies for special education services unless you have been duly notified of the meeting and given reasonable opportunity to attend. Also, no meeting can be held for the purpose of altering your child's individual educational programming unless the same conditions have been met.

There may be people at the table who are "experts" about teaching children, there may be people at the table who are "experts" in social skills training, and there may be people at the table who are "experts" on this and "experts" on that. Don't be intimidated. You are the only one at the table who is the definitive expert on your child. You know your child better than anyone else at the table. You know what triggers a tantrum. You know better than anyone else at the table which disciplining approaches work, and what disciplining approaches do not work. You know the things that frustrate your child, and you know the things that push her into a meltdown. You know better than anyone else at the table what helps your child regain control. You are the only one at the table who knows your child's past accomplishments, her interests, and those things at which she is exceptional. Your expertise in these areas is an invaluable asset to the team. Finally, and most important, you are the only person at the table who has a life-long commitment to and an unconditional love for the child.

> **KEY CONCEPT**
>
> As the child's parent, you are the key member of the team.

ROUTE 2: QUALIFYING FOR SPECIAL EDUCATION SERVICES UNDER THE OTHER HEALTH IMPAIRMENT CATEGORY

If your child is struggling at school but does not meet the strict guidelines for getting special services and accommodations under the emotionally disturbed category, there are two other routes for that you and the school might explore for getting your child the services he or she needs to be successful.

Some children who are defiant and/or present chronic behavior problems qualify for services under the Other Health Impaired category. They qualify when their defiance and noncompliance is not the only issue. In addition to their defiance, they have another disorder. For example, about 30 percent of the children who are defiant also have Attention-Deficit/Hyperactivity Disorder (ADHD).[66] If the school deems that the child's ADHD is impairing his or her educational performance, the child may be provided special education services under the Other Health Impairment category. Similarly, schools may provide special education services to children diagnosed as having an anxiety disorder or having depression, conditions that sometimes occur in conjunction with defiant oppositional behavior.

If you think your child might have ADHD, an anxiety disorder, depression, or other behavior disorder, have the child seen by your family physician. If the physician diagnoses such a disorder, the school is obligated to consider the information and how it is affecting your child's educational performance.

ROUTE 3 TO ADDITIONAL SERVICES

There is yet a third route to getting additional services to children with chronic behavior problems. This route is known in education as a 504 Plan. Among other disabilities, a 504 Plan includes children whose learning is substantially impacted by their behavior problems. For example, if your child is not typically completing deskwork, is frequently being removed from class for behavioral reasons, or refuses to comply with instructive directives, the school may decide that he or she qualifies for a 504 Plan. Many defiant oppositional children who are struggling in the classroom qualify for a 504 Plan. However, for a 504 Plan a medical documentation of a specific disorder is required.

SERVICES AND ACCOMMODATIONS

When it is determined that your child qualifies for additional services under any of the three possible routes, the most important question becomes what services and accommodations does your child need? To answer that question, go back and look at the problems that kicked off this process in the first place. For example, your child could have:

- Trouble listening when the teacher is giving information or instructions.
- Difficulty keeping focused on and attending to her deskwork.
- Problems turning in homework on time.
- Challenges getting along with peers.
- Disputes with the teacher because of refusal to follow directives.

The IEP should spell out how each of the child's problems will be addressed. For example:

- Listening: The teacher gives the child an outline of the main concepts being taught. If teaching math, the teacher gives the child a sample problem, showing how it is solved.
- Desk work: Allow the child to go to a study carrel at the back of the room when doing desk work.
- Homework: The child goes to a resource room at the end of the day to get assistance with taking the right homework home along with the right materials and an explanation to the parents as to what needs to be done.
- Spats: Place the child in a counseling group for boys in that age range who are also having problems getting along with peers.
- Disputes: Increase the classroom structure and give the student a daily schedule and work routine.

COMMON SERVICES

In order to get appropriate services, you need to know what services are reasonable and appropriate. There isn't one set of services that fits the needs of every child with special needs, but these are some of the most common and useful services.

Paraprofessional. A paraprofessional is someone who works in the classroom under the direct supervision of the certified educator. The paraprofessional could spend at least some of his or her time working directly with your child doing such things as explaining, encouraging, and redirecting so that your child can finish deskwork assignments. As directed by the certified educator, the paraprofessional often provides individualized instruction in content areas that are difficult for the child. Also, a paraprofessional is another set of eyes and ears in the room, often catching small incidents and redirecting them before they have time to become huge incidents. Finally, paraprofessionals can (hopefully gently) remove a child when he or she is not up to meeting the demands of the classroom.

School Counselor. Most children with behavior problems lack basic social skills. They often do not know how to play with other children during recess. They often don't know how to politely request something they want or need. They often cannot read nonverbal cues to do know whether another student is attempting to disengage or is trying to be friendly. Such children often do not know how to control their anger when they are upset. A school counselor can provide these children targeted social skills training in these and other areas.

School Psychologist.   Among other things, school psychologists assist the classroom teachers in modifying the curriculum and instruction to better meet the child's unique learning needs. Also, the school psychologist may help design a positive behavior support plan, setting the conditions the child needs to display appropriate behavior. Finally, the school psychologist might design and help implement interventions to help the staff respond effectively when the child is having behavior problems.

Speech and Language Therapist.   Many children with challenging behaviors have problems understanding receptive language (what is said to them) and/or using language to express themselves. Among other problems, these children often cannot correctly identify and accurately label their own feelings. This skill is important because the words that we use guide our thinking. If a child has only one feeling word and that word is mad, he or she tends to respond to every emotion-provoking situation as if he or she was mad. Many speech and language therapists are expanding their role to help these children learn to identify their feelings and give their feelings the right label, which decreases their aggressive behavior.

Evaluation of Student Performance.   The child's education team, of which you are a member, should also decide how the student is to be evaluated on his or her schoolwork, and how that evaluation will be reflected on the child's report card. Schools vary widely on how they approach this problem, and there does not seem to be one best answer.

CASE MANAGEMENT

If your child qualified for additional services and accommodations because of behavior problems, you need to know that there probably is no quick fix. Even when these children get excellent services, their well-established patterns of aggressive behavior do not suddenly vanish. Your child probably will need special education services for several successive years, possibly up into high school. During that time, many teachers, special educators, counselors, and administrators will come and go. At the beginning of each year, there probably will be new teachers and new personnel guiding your child's education. Initially, they know very little about your child. All too often, no one told them the little "tricks" that allow the child to be successful at school or the small things that trigger major outbursts. Therefore, you must become your child's long-term case manager.

As the long-term case manager, you have two roles. One role is the keeper of records. You may need a big, three-ring binder with section dividers. One section is for medical information pertaining to the child's developmental history, chronic health problems, and any pertinent accidents or illnesses. If you do not remember your child's health history, your family doctor has that information, and it belongs to you. For the cost of making photocopies and possibly just a little more, you can get a copy of any such pertinent medical records for the your case management file.

Another section of the binder is for evaluations and reports from psychologists, speech therapists, special educators, and other professionals. This section will get thick. Like all sections, it should be filed chronologically, with the most recent information at the front of the section. Finally, you will need a section for the child's IEP goals and progress reports. All of the school-related information that you need is easily gathered. Federal law gives you access to all your child's records maintained by the school.

A given teacher facilitates and tracks your child's progress over one academic year. Then your child typically moves on to the next teacher, who facilitates and tracks your child's progress through that academic year. But no one person systematically tracks your child's progress over his or her entire school career. You need to do this. Not only do you track your child's progress from year to year but, as needed, you bring that information to the attention of your child's educational team. Accordingly, meet with the child's new teacher at the beginning of each academic year to share useful information about your child. A one-page summary sheet that you can leave with the teacher is useful. This is a summary sheet that one parent prepared:

Summary Sheet

Jason _____	September 1 Third Grade

Interests:	Dinosaurs, computer games, soccer.
Strengths:	Likes to help adults one on one, can look after himself in the community. Has a large fund of information and is curious.
Behaviors:	Not completing deskwork, aggressive with peers, outbursts in the classroom.
Triggers:	Being TOLD what to do in a loud stern voice.
	Too much work in too little time. He can't stand not getting finished.
	Sudden changes in the daily routine, such as listening to a guest speaker during regularly scheduled reading time.
What Works:	Leave the room to calm down. Will do so if it is offered or if given gentle assistance. If TOLD to leave the room or firmly escorted, might collapse to floor and have a temper tantrum.
Reading Level:	At the end of May, teacher said he was reading at the 2.6 grade level with good comprehension.
Math Level:	He is good at math. Doing math facts sometimes calms him. At the end of May, his teacher said his math ability was at the 4.2 grade level.
Contact:	Home phone number is 845-5555
	Mother's work phone number is 642-5555
	Dad's work phone number is 345-5555

DISCIPLINE

Your child's educational team should address three discipline issues. The first issue is what positive behavior support plan will be implemented so the child has the conditions that promote positive, socially appropriate behavior. The second issue is how are educators going to intervene if your child displays a target behavior? For example, what does the teacher do when the child adamantly refuses to do any desk work? Or how should the teacher respond when the child gets angry and tips over her desk? Finally, what consequence, if any, should your child experience for displaying a particular target behavior? As a team member, you should be a participant in these discussions so that plans are developed that you support.

The importance of your participation in the development of the discipline plan is underscored by the following two cases. One case was a second-grade boy who moved during the summer to a small town in the upper Midwest. Before school even got started, the 7-year-old came to the community's attention when he used a BB gun to shoot out the windows in expensive RV. Before he was caught for that vandalism, the boy set several fires in abandoned buildings around town. Among other things, the court referred the child to the local mental health center for a psychiatric evaluation. The 7-year-old was diagnosed as having Oppositional Defiant Disorder and Attention-Deficit/Hyperactivity Disorder. Knowing the child would be attending school that fall, the principal requested the records from his previous school in an adjacent state. The records revealed that when in kindergarten, the boy had been expelled for ninety days. In the first grade, the principal expelled the boy for a total of sixty school days. In doing so, the principal probably violated the federal law affording the child the right to an appropriate education. The principal got away with this because the parents did not meet with the principal to advocate for their son.

The other case was a middle school student. He was also diagnosed as having Oppositional Defiant Disorder. This young man adamantly refused to do his desk work. Since testing revealed that the child was capable of doing the work, the educators decided that they would punish him into doing his desk work. They started by taking away lunch privilege. When that did not work, they took away the one class the boy really enjoyed—physical education. Next, they took away another privilege, and another, and so it went. The more privileges the educators took away from the boy, the more entrenched the boy became in his refusal to do any desk work. This power struggle progressed to the point that the student was in a bare room with six easy worksheets to complete. The student was told that when he completed those six worksheets, he could regain all of the privileges that had been taken away. He sat in that room for two weeks, daily refusing to even pick up his pencil.

These two cases make it clear that you need to pay attention to how the school disciplines your child. You have a right to participate in the development of the school's plan to discipline your child. Exercise it!

SCHOOL–PARENT COLLABORATIVE DISCIPLINE PLANS

As you participate in the development of your child's discipline plan, the teacher might offer an idea. The educator may want to collaborate with you on a plan to increase a specific behavior—like completing deskwork assignments. "I think," the teacher might say, "that if we work together, we can improve your child's ability to get her deskwork completed. Starting next Monday, I will give your child a token each time she hands in a deskwork assignment. If she has ten tokens by the end of the week, you can take her out for ice cream on Saturday afternoon. Knowing how much she likes ice cream, I am absolutely certain she will work really work hard to complete her deskwork to earn the reward."

What could be better than your child completing more of her deskwork? So it is tempting to say, "Yes. We will do that." DON'T. It just does not work for parents to collaborate with a teacher on a reward plan. Collaborative reward plans fail because of breakdowns in the home–school communication. For example, it could happen that the child did not earn her tokens. Yet, on Saturday she had ten tokens and wanted to go for ice cream. Not knowing that their daughter found a source for getting tokens just like the ones the teacher dispensed, the parents took her to get ice cream. The teacher saw them in the ice cream store. Understandably, the teacher felt that the parents undermined the agreed upon reward system.

Alternatively, the teacher might suggest that the parent punish the child for naughty behavior at school. For example, the teacher might say, "Latisha pushes other children when she feels that they are in her way. Just yesterday, Amelia was standing in the doorway to the room and Latisha remembered that she had forgotten her book bag in the library. Rather than say, "Please let me by," she pushed Amelia, and she pushed Amelia so hard that Amelia fell and hit her head on the corner of door frame, cutting a big gash in her head. Latisha simply has to stop pushing other children!

So this is what I would like to do. If Latisha pushes one more child, I will immediately phone you. As soon as Latisha gets home, I want you to send her to her room. Except for coming out of her room for supper, she needs to stay there for the rest of the evening. I am certain that if you help me with this, Latisha will stop pushing other students!"

Again, the teacher's plan sounds reasonable. What parent wants her daughter pushing and bullying other students? But while it might be tempting for the parents to support the teacher with her plan to punish Latisha—DON'T!

What if that evening the family had planned to go to Grandmother's to celebrate her 80th birthday? Not wanting to punish Grandmother, the parents tell Latisha that she will not be punished that particular evening, but will be punished the next evening. Sounds good—so far.

The next day in school, the teacher overheard Latisha telling a friend that she went to Grandmother's house last evening and had cake and ice cream! That was not the whole story. But it is what the teacher heard, and the teacher felt betrayed.

> ## KEY CONCEPT
> You should not punish or reward your child for acts he or she did or did not do at school.

The lines of communication between parents and teachers are not sufficient for the two parties to enter into contracts where one party (the teacher) gives the other party (the parents) directives about when it is appropriate either to reward or to punish the child. So if a teacher makes such a proposal to you, decline. Say, "We believe that it is best for the school to handle incidents at school, and we will handle incidents that occur at home."

HELPING YOUR CHILD SUCCEED AT SCHOOL
HOMEWORK

Children who are behaviorally challenged often have trouble getting their deskwork and their homework completed and turned in on time. All of those zeros get recorded in the grade book, and they bring down the child's overall grade to failing. If this is the case with your child, there are three things you can do to help.

As per the suggestion in Chapter 2, schedule a family quiet time. This is a time when the entire family engages in quiet activities and projects. The television is off. There is no company in the house. Older sister is not on the telephone. This household-wide quiet time makes it conducive for the child to do her homework.

You can help your child organize her homework each evening. When children who struggle with homework look at the evening's work, they see a humongous daunting pile of papers and books, and they feel over-whelmed. They are often so overwhelmed that they are defeated before they start. And they don't start. Break your child's homework into doable sizes and give positive feedback and brief breaks after each small section is completed. For example, Mrs. Harding saw that her fourth-grade son, John, had about forty minutes of homework, an amount that would have overwhelmed him. So she separated the homework into three smaller piles. "Let's start with this math worksheet," she said. "It is ten problems. If you need my help, let me know. When you are done, I'll look it over." When John finished the ten math problems, he took a break while his mother looked over the math worksheet to ensure it was completed. "Very good!" she said, handing him the next small bit of homework.

For some children, homework goes like this: "How was your day?" Dad asks his daughter as the family sits down to supper.

"Good," the daughter replies.

"Do you have any homework this evening?"

"Nope," the child reports.

In fact, the girl did have homework. She just didn't remember that the teacher assigned homework. Even if the conversation jogged her memory, it made no difference. The homework was at school.

If that describes your child, you can help. Meet with the teacher to set up a homework log. The teacher or the para-educator fills the log out and gives it to the student at the end of each school day, also making sure the student gets out the door with the necessary materials and books. If there is no homework that day, this is noted in the communication log. At the end of each evening, you should note in the log how homework time went. It is particularly important to tell the teacher why a given assignment did not get completed. For example, sometimes family emergencies and other pressing events happen. That is normal. When it is explained, the teacher will understand. What the teacher will not understand is when the homework comes back uncompleted and without any explanation.

TEACHER–PARENT COMMUNICATION

Teachers who have a challenging child in their classroom appreciate daily communications from home. The parent tells the teacher about any home events that might affect the child's school day. For example, "We took Sarah to the doctor yesterday. Sarah has an ear infection, and she was put on antibiotics. She might have difficulty hearing in class today, especially if you are standing to her right side when explaining things. She might also get tired or even run a slight fever. If she does, it is okay to send her to the school nurse for Tylenol." The teacher will appreciate this information. Knowing it, the teacher will be understanding when Sarah asks for a directive to be repeated, puts her head down on the desk when she should be doing a math worksheet, or asks to stay in from recess.

TROUBLE AT SCHOOL

From time to time, you are likely to get a phone call from either the classroom teacher or the school secretary telling you about some horrible thing your behaviorally challenged child did that day in school. Of course, you are livid that your child could do such a thing. You are also embarrassed. After all, your child should know better than that! You are sorely tempted to meet your child at the door and give him what he has coming. DON'T.

It is the teacher's job or principal's responsibility to give the child the appropriate consequence for whatever inappropriate behavior the child committed at school, not yours. The child does not need to get another consequence or even an ear full when he gets home. Home should be his sanctuary from the stresses, problems, and the mistakes made at school.

When your errant child comes home, hold out your arms wide. If the child walks into them, give him a comforting hug, saying, "I heard that you had a bad day at school today. I am sorry that happened to you." Your support and understanding make it likely that your child will break down in tears, telling you what happened and how sorry he is about it. If he is up to it, you might even be lucky enough to help him figure out why the horrible thing happened and what he could do differently the next time a similar situation arises.

SCHOOLS THAT FALL SHORT

Occasionally, parents find that the educators at their school are either unwilling or unable to provide the necessary and appropriate services to address their child's needs. If you feel that either situation exists, you can turn to one of two sources for help.

Every state Department of Education has staff whose primary job is to respond to parent complaints about a particular school. One of the staff's functions is to examine the complaint to determine whether the school has adequately met its responsibility to provide your child an appropriate education. Their other function is to mediate disputes between parents and the school.

The other source of help is Protection and Advocacy. Anticipating that some agencies would not provide appropriate services to people with disabilities, the federal government established the Protection and Advocacy Service, often called P&A.[67] There is a Protection and Advocacy Office located in the capital of each state with branch offices in nearly every medium-sized community within your state. Its toll-free phone number can be obtained from the Internet or the local phone directory.

> **KEY CONCEPT**
>
> If needed, you can contact the state Department of Education or the Protection and Advocacy Service. Look on the Internet to find phone numbers.

Personnel from P&A will listen to your concerns. If the advocate feels that the school is not complying with federal laws that afford your child an appropriate education, P&A will arrange for a meeting with the appropriate people from the school, and you will be asked to attend. The typical outcome is that the school starts providing the appropriate education to which your child is entitled.

CONCLUSION

Most children with behavior problems struggle at school with peer relationships, teacher relationships, and academics. So don't send your child
to school and hope for the best. Instead, anticipate that your child will
need your assistance. Initiate contact with the school, talking to the building principal and your child's teacher to establish a working relationship
that will allow you to be an effective advocate for your child.

Despite your preventive efforts, your child may still have difficulties at
school. If this happens, it may be possible to secure additional services and
accommodations to help your child be successful at school. The school will
welcome your interest in your child's education and will respond without
hesitation to determine whether your child needs and qualifies for additional services and accommodations. Remember, schools are in the business of helping children be successful. They want your child to succeed in
school as much as you do.

APPLICATIONS

If a child with conduct problems is to succeed in school, it is imperative that parents work closely with the school. Your child needs your emotional support at home for the frustrations and problems she faces daily at school. And she will also need you to liaison with the school and advocate for her. You can do this because you hold key information about your child that the school must know in order to develop an understanding of your child and her needs.

1. Establishing a relationship with school personnel: You might get a call from the school some time during the first few weeks of school, asking for volunteers. It is understood that many parents work outside the home so volunteer activities are varied to fit parents' schedules. Think about the potential activities below and determine whether it is feasible for you to volunteer.

I will volunteer for (check one or two)
___ Playground helper   ___ Sharing a hobby or interest
___ Cafeteria helper   ___ Reading to students
___ Parent Teacher Association ___ Putting student artwork up
___ Fund raising   on the walls
___ Assisting with art projects ___ Helping with a field trip
___ Bringing treats for social
    events

If the school does not take the initiative in asking for volunteers, it would be appropriate to send a note such as the following to your child's teacher:

> I am a parent who values a good relationship between the home and school. Is there something that I could do to help you in the school or in the classroom this year such as
> _____ _____ (list your interests from above or other ideas that you have as to how you can support the work of the teacher)? I can be available on _____ (i.e., Mondays from 2:30 to 3:00 every other week).

2. Initiating a conference with your child's teacher: Parent–teacher conferences are usually scheduled with every parent some time in November after the first nine weeks of school is completed. Parents of defiant children cannot wait that long before conferencing with their child's teacher. It is best to request a conference within the first two weeks of school. The purpose of the conference is to build a positive relationship with the teacher and share information about your child that may help your child get off to a good start. Do not assume that information shared with the school the previous academic year has been shared with the new teacher.

Prepare this worksheet about your child's strengths, behavior, and any relevant medical issues in preparation for the conference:

Strengths

What is your child particularly good at? Where and when does your child really shine? It is helpful to school personnel to know this in order to establish a positive relationship with your child and set a good tone for the new school year.

My child's behavior is best when he/she is involved in these activities:

_____

_____

My child is good at:

_____   _____   _____

_____   _____   _____

Behavior

The school is going to want to know about the techniques that you have found useful for responding to your child's episodes of noncompliance and defiance. Chances are that your child will recognize and respond to a familiar approach when it is used consistently between the home and the school.

List out the techniques that you have tried from this book that have worked best for you and your child in dealing with defiant behavior:

_____ from Chapter ____ pages _____
_____ from Chapter ____ pages _____

Feel free to make a copy of those sections of the book to share with your child's teacher.

3. Sharing medical information with the school: Many defiant children use medications to help them with impulse control and activity levels. Those medications are often adjusted by physicians at the beginning of a new academic term to take into account the growth and development of the child. The physician will want you to work closely with the school to monitor how the medication is working. You will need to initiate this conference prior to the first day of school or no later than the first week of school. School personnel typically start working at least a week before the students arrive. A sample note is listed below.

> My son/daughter _____ has some medical conditions that could impact his or her learning and behavior. I would like to set up a meeting with you and the _____ (choices could be the counselor, nurse, principal, or school psychologist) to review his/her medical history prior to the start of school.

- Bring the medication bottle with instructions with you.

- Bring a copy of the information from the pharmacy listing any potential side effects.

- Bring any report the physician has given you regarding the diagnosis and treatment.

- If you are comfortable, bring the contact information of the physician and be prepared to sign a release of information form to allow the school principal to talk directly to the physician.

To help you focus the conference, answer the question below.

I want to be certain the school understands these two implications regarding my child's medical condition:

_____

_____

4. Preparing for a conference: In parenting a child who is noncompliant and defiant, there possibly will be a time when you are asked to come to school to deal with an unpleasant incident related to your child's defiant behavior. It sometimes helps to list out the opening questions that you want to ask the teacher or other school personnel to set a positive tone for the meeting and to let the school know you are interested in working with them in a collaborative way. The following list of questions might help you develop a collaborative dialog with the school. Pick a few questions that may work for you.

- What times of day does my child do the best? What times of the day are the most challenging?

- What approaches have worked best for you in dealing with child conduct problems?

- Would you like to know more about approaches that work best for us at home in dealing with conduct problems?

- Which adults in the school does my child seem to relate well to?

- Would it be helpful to elicit their support in working with my child?

9

Venturing into the Community

The Time the Cops Came

"It was nearly a year ago," Mrs. Wong related to the parent-training group, "but I still nearly die from embarrassment when I think about the temper tantrum that Clifford threw at the shopping mall. We had gone to the mall to do some Christmas shopping. It was supposed to be a fun outing. And it was fun while Clifford and I selected Christmas gifts for his two sisters. He was even excited to help pick out hunting boots for his dad. Then we walked by the bicycles. I knew that Clifford wanted a bike for Christmas, so we stopped to look them over. Clifford saw one that he liked. 'Yes,' I told him, 'it's possible that you might get that for Christmas,' and I started to leave.

"'I want it!' Clifford yelled at the top of his lungs.

"'Yes.' I told him, 'But not now. You will get it for Christmas.'

"But Clifford did not understand this. In his eyes, everyone's Christmas gift was in the shopping cart, but his Christmas gift wasn't. I can't begin to tell you the temper tantrum he threw. I had to carry him kicking and screaming out of the store. In the parking lot, he tried to run back into the store, almost getting hit by a car. I had to grab him and hold him down. Then the police came. Someone had told them a mother was in the parking lot beating up her kid."

Nearly every parent of a defiant child can add his or her story to Mrs. Wong's, possibly even topping it. As a result of these horrendous experiences, many parents leave their defiant child home when they go out into the community. Their decision is a understandable, but it is regrettable. Going into the community is a social skill that every child needs to learn. If your defiant child does not have this skill, you need to teach it to him or her.

Successful outings into the community can happen. But in order for these community outings to be successful, they have to be carefully planned. There are seven keys to having a successful outing into the community:

1. The child needs a purpose for being there.
2. Identify the behaviors that are unacceptable.
3. Anticipate what will set off those unacceptable behaviors (the antecedents).
4. Develop a plan to manage these antecedents.
5. Develop a logical consequence that will happen immediately if an unacceptable behavior occurs.
6. Inform your child of the behaviors that are not acceptable and the logical consequences.
7. Review the unacceptable behaviors and the logical consequences at the beginning of the community outing and possibly at key times during the outing.

It will be useful to examine how these seven keys to a successful community outing are applied to places in the community that you are likely to take your child.

THE GROCERY STORE

1. HAVE A PURPOSE

When you take your child into the grocery story, it is not realistic to think that she is going to tag along while you go down aisle after aisle putting groceries in your cart. The child has to have a purpose for being there.

Looking at the grocery store trip from the child's perspective, she must have a reason for being in the grocery store, and reason means an activity. The child must do something meaningful. She must have a series of tasks to occupy her attention.

At a grocery store, the child can be given the task of finding specific food items. If she is capable, her task can also include getting the item from the grocery store shelf and putting it in the grocery cart. Even preschool children can find one grocery item in every aisle. As you now know, defiant children do not like to be told what to do, under any circumstance. So you may need to make the request for grocery items without giving a verbal directive. With a little advance planning, you can have cards prepared for each grocery item that you want the child to find in the grocery store. The cards are the label taken off of the food item and pasted to a piece of cardboard. For example, the front of a macaroni and cheese box is cut out and pasted onto a 4 × 3 piece of light cardboard. The label from a can of green beans is removed and pasted to another 4 × 3 piece of light cardboard. In addition to avoiding a verbal directive, the label makes it easy for the preschool child to go down the aisle and find the green beans, get the right brand, and bring back the right size can. She simply has to match the label in her hand with a can in that aisle that has the same label. Of course, the child's work must be modulated with a healthy dose of common sense. You should not send your child after any item in a glass container or after any item in a stack where removing one of the items can cause the whole stack to crash to the floor.

Thus prepared, as you enter a particular grocery store aisle, hand the child one card, directing her to find one item and, if she is capable, to get the item from the shelf and bring it back to the grocery cart.

Children 7 and older probably do not need a card system. Before going to the grocery store, you and the child can prepare a "treasure hunt," which is the list of grocery items that you want her to find in the grocery store. However, that treasure hunt list has to be carefully managed or else the child will be running all over the store looking for things before you get halfway down the first aisle. So, once the treasure hunt list is prepared, cut it into sections that correspond with the items to be found in each grocery store aisle. Thus, when your child finds her designated items in grocery store aisle and gets them in the grocery cart, she needs to get the next items from you. Of course, you hand her this section of the list as you turn the corner and have clear view of entire aisle. In this way, you will always be able to keep your child in sight without having to give a verbal reprimand.

2. IDENTIFY THE UNACCEPTABLE BEHAVIORS

There are two unacceptable behaviors that a child might display in a grocery store. The child might run out of her parent's view, and the child might have a temper tantrum. Running out of your view is unacceptable because nowadays a young child who runs out of his parent's eyesight in a public place is not safe. A temper tantrum is unacceptable because it deprives other shoppers of their right to have a pleasant shopping experience. A temper tantrum also drives customers from the store, depriving the store owner of income.

3. ANTICIPATE LIKELY ANTECEDENTS FOR THE UNACCEPTABLE BEHAVIORS

The antecedent for children to run away from their parent in the grocery store is boredom. Having nothing to do, they go looking for something to do.

The other unacceptable behavior is a temper tantrum. The thing that sets off a temper tantrum is well known. A temper tantrum is set off when the child decides she wants something that the parent either cannot afford or does not want the child to have.

In this regard, grocery stores conspire against parents. As you go through the checkout line of every grocery store, you are squeezed up against two racks of merchandise. One rack of merchandise is at an adult's eye level. This rack contains magazines and tabloids. You did not come into the grocery store intending to buy that magazine, but while waiting on the checkout line, a spicy caption on the cover catches your attention. Having nothing better to do, you pick up the magazine to "glance" at the article. Oops. It's suddenly your turn to have your groceries scanned. The store clerk looks at you, and she looks at the open magazine in your hand. You have been had. Too embarrassed to put the magazine back, you buy it. "Besides," you rationalize to yourself, "I want to finish reading the article."

The other rack of merchandise in the checkout line has been strategically positioned to be at your child's eye level. As the child impatiently stands in the checkout line, she also has nothing to do. Inevitably, her eyes are drawn to candy bars. "Can I have a candy bar?" the child pleads, grabbing one off of the shelf and holding it up. She knows that if her mother says, "No," all she has to do is look like she is going to have a temper tantrum, and her mother will buy her the candy bar to avoid the threatened public embarrassment.

This scenario is played out hourly in every grocery store in the country, and it has an unfortunate downside. The downside isn't that the child gets the candy bar. Rather, the downside is *how* the child got the candy bar. The child got it by threatening to behave badly, and was promptly reinforced for threatening to have a temper tantrum

4. DEVELOP A PLAN TO DEAL WITH THOSE ANTECEDENTS

The antecedent for the child running out of your view is boredom. However, you have dealt with that antecedent. You have one or two grocery items in each aisle that the child needs to find and put in the grocery cart.

Some grocery store managers are sensitive to the problem that a rack of candy in the checkout line stresses parents, so these stores have one or two candy-free checkout lines. If your store does not provide this, you must outsmart the devious grocery store. It's not hard. Here's how. First, you must accept a fundamental truth about shopping. All shoppers expect to buy something, and often it's something that they really don't need. Think about your last trip to the grocery store. You probably bought ice cream, cookies, or that magazine. Children are no different. When they go shopping, they too expect to buy something. Don't deny it or fight it. Expect to buy the child something.

Before going to the grocery store, ask your child what one special thing she wants, giving her a choice among two or three acceptable items. "Do you want an ice cream sandwich? Do you want a candy bar? Or do you want a chocolate donut?"

The special thing that the child wants to buy goes on the grocery list, but it is last thing purchased. So if the child wants an ice cream sandwich, an ice cream sandwich is the very last thing purchased in the grocery store. Furthermore, the ice cream sandwich does not go in the grocery cart. Rather, the child carries the ice cream sandwich as she goes through the checkout line, giving it up only long enough for the clerk to run the ice cream sandwich across the scanner. This way, your child is not tempted by the candy bars.

5. DEVELOP A LOGICAL CONSEQUENCE

The logical consequence for running away in the store or for having a temper tantrum is leaving the store—immediately! It is likely that you have to employ this logical consequence at least once. If you do, there are two critical elements. The first critical element is that you do not give second chances. For example, if the child runs out of the parent's sight, the parent should not run and find her, and then say, "Now remember, you're not to run out of Mommy's sight." You absolutely cannot do this! If you do, your child will just keep running out of your sight again and again. Why not? Your bark has no bite, and your child knows it.

The second critical element is what you need to do to impose the logical consequence. First, you will have to abandon your grocery cart and the items in it. Sometime before leaving the store, simply inform the store employee about the cart along with a real short explanation of why you are leaving the store. Second, there is no need to create a scene right in the store. Simply take your child by the hand and without explanation or emotion, head for the exit. When you get outside or, better yet, home, then you can explain to your child why you left the grocery store.

However, the best laid plans sometimes go astray. As soon as you take your child by the hand and start walking toward the exit, the child might realize that she is about to be taken out of the store. Of course, that means she will not get to buy that longed-for candy bar. In response, she collapses to the floor and refuses to move. If that happens, you will need to pick her up and carry her kicking and screaming out the door. While that will be terribly embarrassing, it has to be done. For the alternative is letting your child get rewarded for having a temper tantrum, and rewarding a child for bad behavior is absolutely the worst thing you can do. It is never, never worth the few moments of peace that you buy.

6. Inform the Child of the Behaviors That Are Unacceptable

Before leaving for the grocery store, discuss with your child the behaviors that are not acceptable in the grocery store and what will happen if she displays those behaviors. Mrs. Wong had the following discussion with Clifford.

Their Discussion

"Clifford," Mrs. Wong said, "Do you remember what special thing you are going to get in the grocery store?"

"Of course. I'm going to get a Baby Ruth candy bar."

"Yes, you are going to get that candy bar! But there are two things that children sometimes do in the grocery store that they shouldn't. What do you think those two things are?"

"I don't know," Clifford replied, his eyes widening in apprehension.

"Well, one thing is running out of their mother's sight. It is not safe for you to be where I cannot see you. The other thing that children should not do in the grocery store is yell and scream. The store owner likes a nice pleasant grocery store where people like to come shop. He does not like children to yell and scream. Will you be able to go on this shopping trip to the grocery store without running away from me and without yelling and screaming?"

"Yes," Clifford replied, looking at his mother as if she had just asked the dumbest question in the world.

"Good!" But if it should happen, you should know that we will be immediately leaving the grocery store."

7. Review Expectations for Behavior

After parking her car in front of the grocery store, Mrs. Wong asked Clifford these three questions:

- What one thing do you want to get in the store that is just for you?
- If you want to get that (candy bar), what are two things must you not do?

- What will happen if you run away from me or if you start to scream and yell?

A CAR RIDE

Most defiant children cannot ride in a car for longer than fifteen minutes without creating a disruption that makes the trip unpleasant for everyone and possibly even unsafe. However, systematically applying the seven keys to a successful outing can make the difference between a disastrous car ride and a pleasant trip.

1. HAVE A PURPOSE

It is tempting to say that the purpose of a car ride is getting there. But getting there is the adult's purpose for the car ride, not the child's. From the child's point of view, a purpose means having meaningful things to do during the car ride. For any car ride longer than fifteen minutes, defiant children need a sequence of activities. For example, consider a three-hour car ride—a daunting task for any 8-year-old, never mind a behaviorally challenged one. Clearly, a defiant child needs a purpose for being in the car.

Let's consider how to give a sense of purpose for an 8-year-old behaviorally challenged girl who is about to take a three-hour drive to her grandmother's house for the holidays. The other passengers in the car are her dad, who will be driving, and her 14-year-old sister. Both girls will sit in the back seat, where they can spread out and each have a window. A plausible plan to give the girl a purpose for being in the car would be a set of activities, no one of which lasts longer than thirty minutes, following a tentative timeline.

1:00   Depart: It will take everyone fifteen minutes to get settled into trip.

1:15   Alphabet Game: Everyone in the car plays the alphabet game. In this game, you look at signs that can be seen from the car to find the letters of the alphabet, starting with A. Only the first person to see that specific letter in a particular word can use it. For example, the sign reads: *Game Crossing Ahead*. The first person to see the A in *Game* is the only one who can use the A, and then begins searching for a B. But anyone who noticed that *Ahead* also had an A could use that one A.

The Alphabet Game is a good game to play with an adult and one child. But it is a little more complicated when playing with two children with different reading abilities. It is not a good game for a family with children of differing ages. The older children will recognize the shape and color of signs from a distance. Even without being close enough to read the sign, they know what it says and start checking off letters. For example, upon sight of the golden arches, and the teenager in car announces that she has letters C and D. If the defiant child is the younger sibling, as is the situation in this case, she cannot compete with her older sister, and she will have an outburst. Recognizing that this will happen, Dad teams with the 8-year-old girl, pitching in just enough to keep both children within one or two letters of each other. The alphabet game is usually good for about thirty minutes.

1:45   Book Tape: Listen to a book tape that will interest both children. The tape lasts thirty minutes.

2:15   Animal Hunt: The youngest girl, the one with the challenging behaviors, is given a deck of cards showing pictures of five animals that the family can expect to see from the road. The child looks out the window to find each animal. Depending on the area of the country, plausible animals to search for are a dog, a cow, a bird, a cat, and a horse. Finding these five animals usually takes about thirty minutes.

2:45   Snack: This will take an estimated fifteen minutes and can be eaten while the family moves on down the road.

3:00   A Stretch Break: At this point, the car ride has lasted for two hours. That is a long time to sit. Everyone in the car will be ready to stretch their legs, move around, and use the restroom. The break should be planned for and stated in advance so that everyone knows just how long they have to wait. After the stretch break, there is only one more hour to go.

3:15   Singing: Many families are musical, or at least sufficiently musical to sing holiday or other songs that appeal to young children. All of the previous activities had a clear finish. But there is not a clear finish for singing. So a clear finish has to be developed. Either sing a predetermined set of songs, or sing songs for a predetermined amount of time. If singing is not given a clear finish, the defiant child is apt to suddenly announce that she is tired of singing, and isn't going to sing any more. Parents should never allow children to get what they want by behaving badly. So that disaster is avoided by announcing a time limit for the singing. Fifteen minutes is a reasonable time limit for singing.

3:30   Book Tape: Another thirty-minute book tape.

4:00   Now, it is only fifteen minutes to Grandmother's house. This is a good time for everyone to talk about what they want to do at Grandmother's house. It is also a good time to review how people will want to greet Grandmother, where they should put their things when they go into her house. Grandmothers don't like clutter or messes.

2. IDENTIFY THE BEHAVIORS THAT ARE UNACCEPTABLE

When children are traveling in a car, there are two likely behaviors that are not acceptable. One behavior is getting out of the seatbelt. The other behavior is intentionally doing something to irritate a sibling, like kicking the back of her seat.

3. ANTICIPATE THE ANTECEDENTS FOR UNACCEPTABLE BEHAVIORS

One antecedent for irritating a sibling is sitting beside the wrong person during the car ride. For a defiant child, the wrong person is usually the sibling who is next closest in age. If the two of them sit beside each other, it is usually only a matter of time before they start fighting or arguing.

Another antecedent to unacceptable behaviors during car rides is time. Well, it is not time per se. It is the boredom that comes with too much time in the car.

4. DEVELOP A PLAN TO MANAGE THE ANTECEDENTS

Since one antecedent for unacceptable behavior is sitting beside the wrong person, you should establish the seating arrangement that is likely to result in the fewest squabbles among the siblings. The right person for a child with conduct problems to sit beside is usually a parent.

The second antecedent for disruptive behavior during a long car ride is boredom. The planned activities lessen the boredom.

5, 6. Develop a Logical Consequence and Inform Your Child

As mentioned, a logical consequence is necessary when a child is doing things that could hurt someone, break property, or impose on someone else's basic rights. If the child does such things during the car ride, he needs to lose a privilege so everyone is now safe, property will not get broken, and everyone enjoys a pleasant trip. Viewed from that perspective, it is easy to come up with the right logical consequence. If the child gets out of her seatbelt, portends to break anything, or intentionally irritates another passenger, the driver quickly brings the car to a stop. Turning off the engine, the driver rhetorically asks, "Does anyone recall what was said before we started this trip?" Not waiting for an answer, the driver reminds them. "I said that if anyone gets out of the seatbelt or does something that distracts the driver, like starting a fight with your sister, this car comes to a stop. We are now stopped. When everyone is ready to go, let me know."

7. Review Expectations for Behavior

Dad talked with his daughters about the unacceptable behaviors prior to getting into the car. However, a car ride to Grandmother's is a long trip. It is too long for most children to keep the unacceptable behaviors at the forefront of their minds. So from time to time, Dad reviewed the rules. As previously stated, a good way to redirect percolating unacceptable behaviors is to ask the child to self-evaluate. Accordingly, just as agitation started to develop between the defiant child and his sister, Dad asked, "Does anyone remember one of the things we are not going to do on this car ride?"

"Get out of our seatbelt," one child responds.

"Exactly correct. Good memory! And what is the one other thing we are not going to do?"

"Okay, I'll stop poking her."

OLDER SISTER'S BAND CONCERT

Many middle and high school students participate in an extracurricular activity, and all extracurricular activities culminate in some type of public performance. For the sake of making a point, let's say that your daughter plays the flute in the high school band. As sure as trees sprout green leaves in the spring, there will also be a spring band concert. A parent's first thought is that the whole family should go to the band concert. But let's examine that outing from the perspective of the first key to a successful community outing.

1. HAVE A PURPOSE

This family has a 5-year-old son who has challenging behaviors. If the 5-year-old goes the band concert, what is his purpose while at the concert? To listen? That is not an activity. A dead man could appear to listen. Lacking a meaningful activity, the 5-year-old will fidget, squirm, and talk while the band is playing. Eventually, he will do something that will cause his parent to scold him, shush him, or remove him.

If you want to take your child on an outing into the community but cannot think of an activity to keep the child's interest, don't take the child. If the child does not have meaningful activities to do during this outing into the community, he is almost certain to have an outburst. The outburst will embarrass you, it will disrupt the other people who happen to be in this public place, and it will make the child feel badly. Considering what is likely to happen, it is best to either stay home or to get a sitter for the child.

PLAYING WITH FRIENDS

Defiant children must learn how to play with their peers. This is an especially difficult skill for such children who are 5 or 6 years old. To help such a child acquire this skill, it is useful to consider the first five keys to a successful community experience.

1. HAVE A PURPOSE

One would think that the purpose of two children playing together is to have fun. But that is the parents' goal, not the children's. If children are to amicably play together, they must have a clear set of activities. If they don't have a set of activities, the children will either end up in a fight or doing something inappropriate, like seeing how fast the cat can run with a can tied to its tail.

Preschool children's play can be divided into two categories: parallel play and cooperative play. Parallel play is when two children independently do a similar activity. For example, they swing on the swing set or they go down the slide. Parallel play makes the fewest demands on children's social skills. Cooperative play is when the children do a task together. Building a snowman is a cooperative task. Someone has to decide how big the snowman is going to be, and other person has to agree. Chances are, they want to build a humongous snowman. So the children must work cooperatively to roll huge snowballs and to then lift them into place. Someone has to decide how to represent the snowman's eyes, and the other person has to agree. The distinction between parallel play and cooperative play is useful in planning the children's activities. It is best to start the children's playtime with cooperative play, which is the most demanding. As the children get more fatigued and lose their ability to self-monitor their behavior, they should be shifted to parallel play. Accordingly, the following play schedule would be appropriate for two 5-year-old boys:

2:30–3:30	Playtime: Sam comes to our house
2:30	Play catch (using a large foam ball)—cooperative play
2:40	Use Legos to build houses—best done as parallel play activity
2:50	Ride trikes on the sidewalk—parallel play
3:00	Swing on swing set and/or slide down the slide— parallel play
3:15	Snack time—parallel activity
3:30	Sam goes home

2. Unacceptable Behaviors

When 5-year-old children play, three unacceptable behaviors are likely. They get into a fight, something gets broken, or they stop following the established play activities and drift into some type of inappropriate activity.

3, 4. Antecedents and a Plan to Manage Antecedents

There are predictable things that cause young children to fight. One cause is too many children attempting to play together. When three or more children attempt to play together, sides are quickly formed. Sides means that someone is on the outside. The feelings of the child on the outside are hurt. In retaliation, he or she is apt to lash out, perhaps hitting one of the other children or throwing something. So if your child has difficulty playing with peers, invite only one child at a time to come and play.

Another antecedent for fights is unstructured time. But you now have a plan to deal with that antecedent. The children have a sequence of activities.

Finally, children tend to get into fights and arguments at the precarious time when one activity is ending but the next one has not quite started. If transitions between play activities are a problem for your child and her playmate, you will want to be present during these times to direct the children's attention away from the activity that is finishing and toward the activity that you want to get underway. For example, it is time for the children to stop playing catch and switch to building with Legos. You briefly join the game of catch. As the ball goes around this triangle, you foreshadow the end of the catching activity by saying, "Each person has two more catches, and then it will be time to play Legos." When the ball comes to you for the second time, you hold it. Putting it behind your back to put it out of sight, you grab the box of Legos. You dump them out, and hand each child several blocks. This technique for making transitions between play activities works every time.

The second unacceptable behavior that often happens when children play together is that something gets broken. This usually happens because there are too many things out or because the children are playing where they shouldn't be playing or inappropriately with the toys. So put out only what the children need to play with at that particular moment. And guide them to the right place to play. For example, you don't want them playing catch beside your flower bed.

A final consideration is that play, like all other activities, must have a clear finish. In this case, a time limit has been set. When the time for playing has elapsed, the children are called to a high-interest activity, like having a snack.

5. LOGICAL CONSEQUENCE

When children get in a fight or when something is broken intentionally, the logical consequence is that the playtime is over. The friend goes home.

OTHER SITUATIONS

There are other possible outings into the community, but all of them can be done successfully if they are planned on the basis of the seven key principles. But remember that failing to plan is planning to fail.

ACCESSING COMMUNITY RESOURCES

Your community has resources that can assist you and your child. Even in this day of urbanization, there remains more than a grain of truth in the adage: It takes a village to raise a child. So how do you get the village to help?

COMMUNITY YOUTH ACTIVITIES

Nearly all communities have organized afterschool, weekend, and summer programs and activities for young children and adolescents. Community-based sport programs enhance children's physical fitness, develop their motor skills, and teach them how to participate in competitive games. Religious education programs, scouts, Future Farmers of America, and other such organizations not only teach life-long skills, but they support your efforts to teach core values. Encourage and assist your child in getting involved in a few of these programs.

SUPPORT GROUPS

Parent-support groups are also invaluable. It is impossible to overstate how much you can get from being part of a parent-support group. You will find it reassuring to discover that you are not the only one in the world who is raising a child with challenging behaviors. Parents in support groups also learn a lot by listening to other parents tell about how they dealt with this or that situation, and often find that it is just like the one they are currently facing. Finally, it is comforting to be listened to by other parents who know exactly what you are going through.

Several resource sites for parents of defiant children can be found on the Internet. One website is www.conductdisorders.com; another is www.psychcentral.com. Both Internet sites list recommended books and pertinent magazine or journal articles. On the downside, they cover the broad span of childhood behavior problems, and they do not focus exclusively on defiant children. Finally, neither site offers a chat room, which is a place where you can go and "talk" with other parents.

Ideally, you will be able find a support group for parents of defiant children in your community. Ask the counselor or therapist at your community mental health center who specializes in childhood behavior problems if there is such a support group in your community. You could also ask the director of the adolescent psychiatric unit of your local hospital or your child's pediatrician.

However, you might find that no such parent support exists in your community. So start one. You can do this by leaving your name and phone number with several professionals who serve defiant children and their parents. While the professionals will not give out the names of their patients, they will share your name and phone number with others who are in a similar situation. If you attach a little biographical information about yourself, your family, and the age of your child, it will be only a matter of time before some parent calls you. Two can form a support group, and from there it will expand.

CONCLUSION

Children with behavior problems also often have problems on outings into the community. Problems are particularly likely if the outing is not planned. Outings that unfold spontaneously often end up in a disaster for both the child and you. The solution is to invest upfront time to plan the outing, doing every reasonable thing to set the child and you up for success.

APPLICATIONS

Grocery Store

If you are not throughly familiar with the layout of your grocery store, leave the child at home under someone else's supervision and go make a diagram of the store. Record the items that your child would be able to find in each particular aisle, being careful to select the items that are at your child's eye level or lower.

1. Use this information to complete the following chart, writing in the blanks the items in each aisle that you might potentially need and that your child could find, safely get from the store shelf, and put into the grocery cart:

Aisle #1   **Aisle #2**   **Aisle #3**   **Aisle #4**

_____   _____   _____   _____

_____   _____   _____   _____

_____   _____   _____   _____

Aisle #5   **Aisle #6**   **Aisle #7**   **Aisle #8**

_____   _____   _____   _____

_____   _____   _____   _____

_____   _____   _____   _____

2. If your child is 7 or younger, cut out the labels or box fronts of each of these food items. Put the labels and box fronts and the aisle information into a plastic bag.

Prior to departing for the store, go through the plastic bag, selecting the labels and box fronts of items that you need to purchase that day.

3. Prior to leaving for the grocery store, ask your child the one thing he or she would like to purchase at the store. Find a label for that item.

4. If your child is 8 or older, jointly develop a "treasure hunt." At the end of your discussion, ask your child this question: "What behaviors do you have to show in the store?" She almost certainly will be able to answer the question.

5. "That is right. The people at the grocery store do not like it when children _____."

6. Continuing the discussion, say words to this effect, "However, that sometimes happens to you. If that happens, we will leave the grocery cart right where it is and we will quickly leave the store."

Should this happen, do not berate or belittle the child. Simply leave the store. That is the logical consequence, and using the logical consequence is one key tool to helping defiant children.

7. When you take your 7-year-old or younger child grocery shopping, inform your child at the entrance to each aisle how many food items she is to find in that aisle. Then hand her the first label or the box front of the first item to be located in that aisle and put into the grocery cart. When she finds that particular item and gets it into the cart, hand her the next item. Of course, each time retrieve the label and box front, but do not put it in the plastic bag. Instead, put the label or box front of the successfully retrieved item out of sight, such as in your purse or pocket. That way, when the shopping trip is over, all of the items in the plastic bag will be gone. The food-finding task will be "finished."

8. The last item purchased is the child's special item. It works best if the child does not put this item in the grocery cart, but rather hangs onto it except for briefly giving it up so it can be scanned in the checkout line.

Car Ride

If car rides are a problem area, you will want to complete this form to establish a smooth routine for riding in the car. Once the form is completed for a specific car ride, it can be used for similar car rides in the future.

Car Ride

Destination _____   Length of the Ride _____

Seating:

Driver   Right Front Seat

_____   _____

Back Left Seat   Back Right Seat

_____   _____

Back Left Van Seat   Back Right Van Seat

_____   _____

Time	**Activity**	**Length of Activity**
____	_____	_____
____	_____	_____
____	_____	_____
____	_____	_____

Community Youth Activities

1. Pick up a community youth activity brochure at your city's Park and Recreation Department, Chamber of Commerce, public library, YMCA, or church. Read the activity choices with your child and have her circle several of the activities that sound interesting and fun. The activities of interest are:

   _____   _____   _____

   _____   _____   _____

2. An important next step is for you to learn more about the person leading the activities of interest to your child. Just as matching the right teacher for a defiant child is critical to school success, matching the right youth leader is important to your

child's enjoyment and success in adult-supervised community activities.

An indirect way to assess this match is to ask your friends, neighbors, or your child's teacher if they have any information they could share with you about how the leader of a particular activity would work with a child with challenging behaviors.

A more direct approach to assessing this match would be to express your child's interest in the activity, let the organization know that your child has special needs and ask if you could watch about five minutes of the activity to see if this activity would be a good fit for your child. Watch for these things:

> How does the leader greet the participants?
>
> Is the leader organized and on task?
>
> How does the leader handle challenging behaviors?
>
> Is the leader a positive person who genuinely seems to enjoy working with young people?

3. Choose one activity for your child based upon the youth leader who appears to have the best potential for providing a nurturing environment for your defiant child.

10

Parting Advice

Parenting provides a lot of rewards. But parenting can also be hard work. Realizing that most parents reading this book are also working outside the home and caring for other family members, this last chapter is to help you put it all together. One way to manage implementing the suggestions given in this book to help your defiant child is to systematically implement the activities found at the end of each chapter, taking one chapter per month. You can conveniently fit the application activities at the end of each chapter onto a calendar with one "assignment" each week. The calendars on the subsequent pages are sequenced to follow the chapters in the book. Alternatively, you could also pick the chapter that you feel will make the most significant difference for your child and start there.

You get the point. The key is making a commitment to start, and then just doing it. If you faithfully implement a set of activities for even one month, the improvements that you see will motivate you to do the activities for the next month. As the Chinese proverb says, The longest journey begins with a single step.

Month One: Getting Started

Monday	Tuesday	Wednesday	Thursday	Friday	Sat/Sun
			1	2	3
					4
5	6	7	8 Assess your personal stressors and make a plan to reduce Category 1 stressors. (p. 22)	9	10
					11
12	13 Implement one action step of your plan, such as making an appointment with your physician to deal with depression. (p. 23)	14	15	16	17
					18
19	20	21 Implement your plan to get additional child care support. (p. 25)	22	23	24
					25
26	27	28	29 Go on an outing with a friend to celebrate your first steps in beginning to reduce your stress level! (p. 25)	30	

Month Two: Making the House a Home

Monday	Tuesday	Wednesday	Thursday	Friday	Sat/Sun
					1
					2
3	4	5	6	7	8
					9
10	11	12	13 Organize the adults' possessions, including your closets and garage. (p. 43)	14	15
					16
17	18	19 Help your children organize their possessions. (p. 43)	20	21	22
					23
24 Begin structuring key home activities such as meals, family time, and bedtime. Post the schedule. (p. 44)	25	26	27	28	29
31					30

Month Three: Making the House a Home

Monday	Tuesday	Wednesday	Thursday	Friday	Sat/Sun
	1	2	3	4	5 6
7	8	9	10 Inventory your children's exposure to violence in their toys, games, and videos. (p. 44)	11	12 13
14	15	16	17 Make a list of violent items that need to be replaced. Consider a family garage sale!	18	19 20
21	22	23	24 Prepare a list of replacement toys, books, and DVDs from the resource list in Chapter 2. (pp. 48–49)	25	26 27
28	29	30	31 Implement one strategy to enhance the positive atmosphere in your home. (p. 50)		

Month Four: Strengthening the Parent–Child Relationship

Monday	Tuesday	Wednesday	Thursday	Friday	Sat/Sun
					1
2	3	4	5 Assess the nature of your interactions with your child. (p. 65)	6	7 8
9	10	11	12 Find five ways to acknowledge your child's accomplishments. (p. 66)	13	14 15
16	17	18	19 Label your child's behavior during a few activities. (pp. 66–67)	20	21 22
23	24	25	26 Praise your child's behavior in at least two ten-minute time periods. (pp. 67–68)	27	28 29
30	31				

Month Five: Stop Saying, "Stop That!"

Monday	Tuesday	Wednesday	Thursday	Friday	Sat/Sun
		1	2	3	4
					5
6	7	8	9	10	11
		Identify irritating behaviors that can be ignored. (p. 83)			12
13	14	15	16	17	18
		Practice using Alpha Commands to redirect behavior. (p. 84)			19
20	21	22	23	24	25
		Allow your child to experience a natural consequence this week. (p. 85)			26
27	28	29	30		

Month Six: The Value of Routines

Monday	Tuesday	Wednesday	Thursday	Friday	Sat/Sun
				1	2
					3
4	5	6	7 Work together to develop a routine of low-interest and high-interest activities. (p. 104)	8	9
					10
11	12	13 Work together to make a communication borad to implement the routine. (p. 104)	14	15	16
					17
18	19	20 Chart how you helped your child implement the routine. (p. 105)	21	22	23
					24
25	26	27 Chart how you praised and affirmed your child's success in implementing the routine. (p. 106)	28	29	30
					31

Month Seven: Breaking the Coercive Cycle

Monday	Tuesday	Wednesday	Thursday	Friday	Sat/Sun
1	2	3	4	5	6
					7
8	9	10	11 Help your child make a plan to calm him- or herself. (p. 128)	12	13
					14
15	16	17	18 Go with your child to share the plan with at least three people. (p. 128)	19	20
					21
22	23	24 Role-play the plan several times. (p. 128)	25	26	27
					28
29	30	31			
Help your child monitor efforts to implement the plan. (p. 125)					

Month Eight: Rules and Tools

Monday	Tuesday	Wednesday	Thursday	Friday	Sat/Sun
			1	2	3
					4
5	6	7	8 Identify logical consequences for hurting someone or causing property damage. (p. 145)	9	10
					11
12	13	14 Discuss inappropriate behaviors and the logical consequences with your child. (p. 145)	15	16	17
					18
19	20	21 Help your child gain the understanding and skill to eliminate key behaviors. (p. 146)	22	23	24
					25
26	27	28			

Month Nine: Going to School

Monday	Tuesday	Wednesday	Thursday	Friday	Sat/Sun
				1	2
					3
4	5	6	7 Establish a relationship with personnel in your child's school by volunteering. (p. 168)	8	9
					10
11	12	13	14 Initiate a conference with your child's teacher and share information about your child. (p. 169)	15	16
					17
18	19	20 Try one of the homework strategies with your child. (p. 164)	21	22	23
					24
25	26	27	28	29	30

Month Ten: Venturing into the Community

Monday	Tuesday	Wednesday	Thursday	Friday	Sat/Sun
			1	2	3
					4
5	6	7	8 Identify the items at the grocery store that your child could find and put safely in your cart. (p. 189)	9	10
					11
12	13	14 Make your plastic bag with labels and box fronts of items your child will select at the store. (p. 190)	15	16	17
					18
19	20	21 Implement the grocery shopping strategy and be prepared to use your logical consequence with your child. (p. 190)	22	23	24
					25
26	27	28 Implement the car ride strategy, planning activities and using a seating chart. (p.191)	29	30	31

Notes

CHAPTER 1

1. Rey, J. M. (1993). Oppositional Defiant Disorder. *American Journal of Psychiatry, 12,* 1769–1778.

2. Huesmann, L. D., Eron, L. D., Lefkowitz, M. M., & Walder, J. O. (1984). The stability of aggression over time and generations. *Developmental Psychology, 20,* 1120–1134.

3. Comings, D. E. (1997). Genetic aspects of childhood behavior disorders. *Child Psychiatry and Human Development, 27,* 139–150.

4. American Psychiatric Association. (1990). *Diagnostic and statistical manual of mental disorders* (4th ed.) Washington, DC: Author.

5. Biederman, J., Newcron, J., & Sprick, S. (1991). Comorbidity of attention deficit hyperactivity disorder with conduct, depression, anxiety, and other disorders. *Journal of Psychiatry, 148,* 564–577.

6. Monstra, V. J., Monstra, D. M., & George, S. (2002). The effects of stimulant therapy, EEG biofeedback, and parenting style on the primary symptoms of attention-deficit/hyperactivity disorder. *Journal of Psychophysiology and Biofeedback, 27,* 231–249.

7. Webster-Stratton, C. (1990). Stress: A potential disruptor of parent perceptions and family interactions. *Journal of Clinical Child Psychology, 19,* 302–312.

8. Albidin, R. R. (1983). *Parenting stress index: Manual.* Charlottesville, VA: Pediatric Psychology Press.

9. O'Leary, K. D., & Emery, R. E. (1982). Martial discord and child behavior problems. In M. D. Levine & P. Satz (Eds.), *Middle childhood: Developmental variation and dysfunction* (pp. 343–364). New York: Academic Press.

10. Stoneman, Z., Body, G., & Burke, M. (1988). Maternal quality, depression, and inconsistent parenting: Relationship with observed mother-child conflict. *American Journal of Orthopsychiatry, 59,* 105–117.

11. Kim-Cohen, J., Moffit, T. E., Taylor, A., Panbly, S. J., & Casp, A. (2005). Maternal depression and children's antisocial behavior: Nature and nurture effects. *Archives of General Psychiatry, 62,* 173–181.

12. American Psychiatric Association. (1990). *Diagnostic and statistical manual of mental disorders* (4th ed.). Washington, DC: Author.

13. Kennedy, S. H., Lam, R. W., Nutt, D. J., & Thase, M. E. (2004). *Treating depression effectively.* London: Martin Duntiz, distributed in the USA by Taylor & Francis.

14. Steinhauser, H. C. (1996). Children of alcoholic parents: A review. *European Child & Adolescent Psychiatry, 32,* 411–421.

15. Malone, S. M., Iacono, W. G., & McGue, M. (2002). Drinks of the father: Father's maximum number of drinks consumed predicts externalizing disorders, substance abuse, and substance abuse disorders in preadolescent and adolescent offspring. *Alcoholism: Clinical and Experimental Research, 26,* 1823–1832.

16. Wahle, R., & Dumas, J. (1984). Changing the observational coding styles of insular and noninsular mothers: A step toward maintenance of parent training effects. In R. F. Dangel & R. A. Polseter (Eds.), *Parent training: Foundations of research and practice* (pp. 379–416). New York: Guilford Press.

17. Bank, L., Forgatch, M. S., Patterson, G. R., & Fetrow, R. A. (1993). Parenting practices of single mothers: Mediators of negative contextual factors. *Journal of Marriage and the Family, 55,* 371–384.

18. Dubrow, E. F., & Ippolito, M. F. (1994). Effects of poverty and quality of the home environment on changes in the academic and behavior adjustment of elementary school-age children. *Journal of Clinical Child Psychology, 23,* 401–412.

19. Ackerman, B. P., Kogos, J., Youngstrom, E., Schoff, K., & Izard, C. (1999). Family instability and the problem behaviors of children from economically disadvantaged families. *Developmental Psychology, 3,* 246–257.

20. Homel, R., Burns, A., & Goodnow, J. (1987). Parental social networks and child development. *Journal of Social and Personal Relations, 4,* 159–177.

21. Lessenberry, B. H., & Rehfeldt, R. A. (2004). Evaluating stress levels of parents of children with disabilities. *Exceptional Children, 70,* 234–244.

22. Donnenberg, G., & Baker, B. L. (1991). The impact of young children with externalizing behaviors on their families. *Journal of Abnormal Child Psychology, 21,* 179–198.

23. Kazdin, A. (1987). *Treatment of antisocial behavior in children: Current status and future direction.* Homewood, IL: Dorsey.

CHAPTER 2

24. Beals, D. E. (2001). Eating and reading: Links between family conversations with preschoolers and later language literacy. In D. K. Dickinson, E. Pattons, & E. Tabors (Eds.), *Beginning literacy with language: Young children learning in home and school.* Baltimore: Paul H. Brookes.

25. Wildawsky, R. (1994, October). What's behind success in school? *Reader's Digest,* 49–55.

26. Bowden, B. S., & Zeisz, J. M. (1997). *Supper's on! Adolescent adjustment and frequency of family mealtimes.* Paper presented at 105th annual meeting of American Psychological Association, Chicago, IL.

27. Harris, R. J. (1989). *A cognitive psychology of mass communication.* Hillsdale, NJ: Lawrence Erlbaum.

28. Bandura, A., Ross, D., & Ross, S. A. (1961). Transmission of aggression through imitation of aggressive models. *Journal of Abnormal and Social Psychology, 63, 575–582.*

29. Eron, L. D. (1963). Relationship of TV viewing habits and aggressive behavior in children. *Journal of Abnormal and Social Psychology, 64,* 1993–1996.

30. Howitt, D., & Cumberpatch, G. (1975). *Mass media, violence and society.* London, Paul Elck.

31. Philips, D. P. (1986). Natural experiments on the effects of mass media violence on fatal aggression. In R. Berkowitz, (Ed.), *Advances in experimental social psychology.* San Diego: Academic Press.

32. Joy, L. A., Kimball, M. M., & Zabrack, M. L. (1986). Television and children's aggressive behavior. In T. M. Williams (Ed.), *The impact of television: A natural experiment in three communities* (pp. 303–360). Orlando, FL: Academic Press.

33. Huesmann, L. R., Moise-Titus, J., Podolski, C., & Eron, L. D. (2003). Longitudinal relations between children's exposure to TV violence and their aggressive and violent behavior in young adulthood, 1977–1992. *Developmental Psychology, 39,* 201–221.

34. Ahlstrom, W. M., & Havighurst, R. J. (1971). *400 losers.* San Francisco: Jossey-Bass.

CHAPTER 3

35. Bowlby, R. (1956). Mother-child separation. In K. Soddy (Ed.), *Mental health and infant development, Vol 1: Papers and discussion.* Oxford: Basic Books.

36. Bowlby, R. (2004). *Fifty years of attachment theory.* London: Karnac Books.

37. Bowlby, R. (1958). The nature of the child's tie to his mother. *International Journal of Psycho-Analysis, 39,* 350–373.

38. Ainsworth, M. S., Bell, S. M., & Stayton, D. J. (1971). Individual differences in strange situation behavior of one-year-olds. In J. R.

Schaffer (Ed.), *The origins of human social relations* (pp. 17–57). London: Academic Press.

39. Erickson, M. F., Sroufe, L. A., & Egeland, B. (1985). The relationship between quality of attachment and behavior problems in preschool in a high-risk sample. In I. Bretherton & W. Waters (Eds.), Growing points of attachment theory and research. *Monographs of the Society for Research in Child Development, 50,* 147–166. Chicago: University of Chicago Press.

40. Allen, J. P., Hauser, S. T., & Borman-Spurell, E. (1996). Attachment theory as a framework for understanding sequelae of severe and adolescent psychopathology: An 11-year follow-up study. *Journal of Consulting and Clinical Psychology, 64,* 254–263.

41. Bates, J. E., & Bayles, K. (1988). Attachment and the development of behavior problems. In J. Belsky & T. Nezworski (Eds.), *Clinical implications of attachment.* Hillsdale, NJ: Lawrence Erlbaum.

CHAPTER 4

42. Duker, P. C., & Syes, D. M. (1983). Symposium on behaviour modification treatments II: Long-term follow-up effects of extinction and overcorrection procedures with severely retarded individuals. *British Journal of Mental Subnormality, 27*(57, Pt 2), 74–80.

43. Forehand, R., & McMahon, R. J. (1981). *Helping the noncompliant child: A clinician's guide to parent training.* New York: Guilford Press.

44. Perske, R. (1972). Dignity of risk and the mentally retarded. *Mental Retardation, 10,* 24–27.

CHAPTER 5

45. Premack, D. (1954). Reinforcement of drinking by running: Effect of fixed ratio and reinforcement time. *Journal of Experimental Analysis of Behavior, 7,* 91–96.

46. Schopler, E. (1988). *Individual assessment and treatment for autistic and developmentally disabled children.* Baltimore: University Park Press.

CHAPTER 6

47. Patterson, G. R. (1989). *Coercive family process*. Eugene, OR: Castilia.

48. Riley, D. A. (1997). *The defiant child: A parent's guide to oppositional defiant disorder*. New York: Guilford Press.

49. Dobson, J. (2004). *The strong-willed child: Birth through adolescence*. Wheaton, IL: Tyndale House.

50. Bjorklund, D. F., & Harnishfeger, K. K. (1995). The evolution of inhibition mechanisms and their role in human cognition and behavior. *Interference and Inhibition in Cognition*, 141–173.

51. Glasser, W. (1965). *Reality therapy: A new approach to psychiatry*. New York: Harper & Row.

CHAPTER 7

52. *History of the Prohibition Act of 1920*. (2002). Retrieved July 15, 2006 from http://www.id.essortment.com/historyprohibition.

53. Van Houten, R. (1983). Punishment: From the animal laboratory to the applied setting. In S. Axelrod & J. Apsche (Eds.), *The effects of punishment on human behavior* (pp. 13–44). New York: Academic Press.

54. Dodson, J. (1992). *The new dare to discipline*. Wheaton, IL: Tyndale House.

55. Azrin, N. H., & Besalel, V. A. (1980). *How to use over-correction*. Lawrence, KS: H & H Enterprises.

56. Weiner, H. (1962). Some effects of response-cost on human operant behavior. *Journal of the Experimental Analysis of Behavior, 5*, 201–208.

57. Bostow, D. E., & Bailey, J. B. (1969). Modification of severe disruptive and aggressive behavior using brief timeout and reinforcement procedures. *Journal of Applied Behavior Analysis, 2*, 31–37.

58. Barkley, R. A., & Benton, C. M. (1998). *Your defiant child: 8 steps to better behavior*. New York: Guilford Press.

59. *History of the Treatment of Mental Illness.* Reviewed March 20, 2007 from http://www.mentalhealthworld.org/29ap.htm

60. Wool, D. I., & Stephens, T. M. (1978). Twenty-five years of caring for and treating feeble-minded person in the United States: A review of the literature from 1874 to 1900. *Journal of Special Education, 12,* 219–229.

61. Lovass, O. I., Schreibman, L., & Koegel, R. L. (1974). A behavior modification approach to the treatment of autistic children. *Journal of Autism & Childhood Schizophrenia, 4,* 111–129.

62. Dreikurs, R., & Grey, L. (1968). *Logical consequences.* New York: Meredith Press.

63. Glaser, W. (1965). *Reality therapy: A new approach to psychiatry.* New York: Harper.

CHAPTER 8

64. Public Law 94–142 (S.6), Education of All Handicapped Children Act of 1975.

65. Individuals with Disabilities Education Act of 2004.

66. Burns, G. L., Walsh, J. A., Gomez, R. N. (2006). Measurement and structural invariance of parent ratings of ADHD and ODD symptoms across gender for American and Malaysian children. *Psychological Assessment, 18,* 452–457.

67. Protection and Advocacy for Individuals Rights (PAIR) under the Rehabilitation Act of 1973.

Index

About the Authors

Philip S. Hall, Ph.D. is a licensed psychologist with 34 years of experience working with children and adolescents who, for one reason or another, struggle to find success. During his professional career, he was the Director of South Dakota's Adolescent Drug Treatment Program, Director of Psychological Services for the Developmental Disabilities Clinic at the University of South Dakota Medical School, Director of the School Psychology Training Program at the University of South Dakota, and Director of the School Psychology Training Program at Minot State University. While at Minot State University, Dr. Hall coordinated with the medical community, the community mental health center, and the public school system to offer a comprehensive clinic for defiant children and their parents. Recently retired from academia, he continues to consult widely. Current projects include assisting two off-reservation, boarding schools for Native American children to move from a discipline model based on punishment to a caregiving model based on instilling discipline. At both schools, the number of behavior incidents have dropped in half, the academic achievement scores have increased, the year-to-year retention rates have increased, and on surveys the students register increased satisfaction and contentment. This book reflects the experiential learning that Dr. Hall has acquired by working with children, their parents, and the agencies that serve them.

Nancy Hall, Ed.D. has worked for the past 27 years in educational administration. Fifteen of those years were as an elementary school principal, where she worked closely with over 500 children a year, their parents, teachers, and community service providers. In that role, she gained considerable experience in guiding aggressive, disruptive, and defiant children. She learned how to help parents and teachers provide an environment and routines in which these children could be successful. She learned how to interact with defiant children in ways that promoted positive behavior. She is currently the Dean of the College of Education at Black Hills State University, providing leadership for the development of the next generation of teachers.

Philip and Nancy Hall are co-authors of *Educating Oppositional Defiant Children*, which is published by the Association of Curriculum and Development (ASCD). The book won the Golden Lamp Award based on the critical educational need addressed and the quality of the writing. The book has remained one of ASCD's best-selling works for the past three years. This book has not only enjoyed success in this country, it has also been translated in Chinese and published there by the China Light Press. The book, numerous related publications, and international presentations have made them recognized as experts in instructing others as to new and useful ways to help defiant children.